My 52 Object Lessons (1)

JOSÉ JÁENZ

For the teaching of the Bible

My 52 Object Lessons (1)

First edition: December 2024

ISBN-13: 9798305113815

Copyright © of the text: José Jáenz

All rights reserved

No part of this book may be reproduced in any form, including electronic, mechanical, photocopying, recording, or any other means, without the prior written permission of the copyright holders. Please contact josejaenz@yahoo.es if you need to photocopy or scan any portion of this work.

Cover: freepik.es

Graphics: freepik.es

Publisher: Independently published

DEDICATION

I dedicate this book of Object Lessons to God, Lord and Creator of all that exists, who has given me life, as well as the ability and willingness to write this book.

I also dedicate this book to all those who love the teaching of the Bible, the word of God, especially to my teachers at APEN Nicaragua, who instilled in me (many years ago) an interest in object Lessons through the training and courses I received.

Additionally, I would like to dedicate it to sister María S. de Eudaly, whom I never met, but who, despite the distance and time, inspired me to write object Lessons after I accidentally discovered a copy of a small book she published in 1962, called Lecciones Objetivas (Objective Lessons).

I also dedicate it to the hundreds of girls and boys I have had the opportunity to teach about the good news of Jesus. For them, I strived to be a good teacher, to communicate God's word in a simple yet effective way. It was through them that the Lord opened my eyes and showed me the need we all share, regardless of age, to know about God's love through His Son, Jesus Christ.

With gratitude and love,

Brother José Jáenz

NOTICE TO THE READER

This book was originally written in Latin American Spanish and has been translated using artificial intelligence technology. While every effort has been made to ensure an accurate translation, there may be errors or phrases that do not accurately reflect the meaning or style of the original text.

If you find any errors in the translation, or words or phrases that you feel are inappropriate, please let us know. Please send an e-mail to the author at josejaenz@yahoo.es, indicating the page number and the error found.

Thank you for your understanding and cooperation.

Brother José Jáenz

CONTENTS

ACKNOWLEDGEMENTS..1

Object Lesson 1: Traffic Sign 2

Object Lesson 2: The Iron 4

Object Lesson 3: The Cell Phone 6

Object Lesson 4: The Soccer Ball. 8

Object Lesson 5: The Life Jacket....................................10

Object Lesson 6: The Airplane. 12

Object Lesson 7: The Microphone.................................14

Object Lesson 8: The Book. 16

Object Lesson 9: Glasses. 18

Object Lesson 10: Sports Shoes.....................................20

Object Lesson 11: Headphones. 22

Object Lesson 12: The Tablet. 24

Object Lesson 13: The Tie..26

Object Lesson 14: The Calendar....................................28

Object Lesson 15: The Fruits. 30

Object Lesson 16: The Tree. 32

Object Lesson 17: The Chair..34

Object Lesson 18: The Bill. 36

Object Lesson 19: Bald boy baby doll. 38

Object Lesson 20: The Trumpet....................................40

Object Lesson 21: The Cross. 42

Object Lesson 22: Water, Ice, and Vapor. 44

Object Lesson 23: The Wig. 46

Object Lesson 24: The Triangle. 48

Object Lesson 25: The Tambourine. 50

Object Lesson 26: The Stethoscope. 52

Object Lesson 27: The Letter. 54

Object Lesson 28: The Couple. 56

Object Lesson 29: The Arrow. 58

Object Lesson 30: The ID Card. 60

Object Lesson 31: The Passport. 62

Object Lesson 32: Credit Card. 64

Object Lesson 33: The Boat. 66

Object Lesson 34: Rubbing Alcohol. 68

Object Lesson 35: The Remote Control. 70

Object Lesson 36: The Battery-Powered Toy. 72

Object Lesson 37: The Dirty Glass. 74

Object Lesson 38: The Candle 76

Object Lesson 39: Salt. 78

Object Lesson 40: Milk. 80

Object Lesson 41: The Rock. 82

Object Lesson 42: The Branch. 84

Object Lesson 43: The Dinosaur. 86

Object Lesson 44: Police Handcuffs. 88

Object Lesson 45: The Face Mask. 90

Object Lesson 46: The Teddy Bear. 92

Object Lesson 47: The Toothbrush. 94

Object Lesson 48: The Box and the Light. 96

Object Lesson 49: The Rod. 98

Object Lesson 50: The Stained Shirt. 100

Object Lesson 51: The Jewels. 102

Object Lesson 52: The Flowers. 104

ACKNOWLEDGEMENTS

I would like to express my deep gratitude to God, who has given me life, health, and the strength to carry out this work.

I also thank my family, especially my wife Dayana, and my daughters Susan and Eliana, for giving me the love and patience needed to dedicate myself to writing.

I would like to thank my brothers and sisters in the faith, especially those who have been an important part of my beginnings in God's work, such as Brother Norman Alonzo, who led me to Christ, and Brother Sergio Torres, who encouraged me to begin teaching the Bible to children.

Finally, I want to thank all the readers who delve into these pages, for their interest and willingness to share with me the experience of teaching God's Word.

With humility and gratitude,

Brother José Jáenz

TRAFFIC SIGN

Object Lesson 1: Traffic Sign

Materials: A traffic sign.

Introduction: Explain to the students the meaning of the traffic sign we have (stop, danger, no parking, etc.). Ask them what would happen if we don't obey the sign. Depending on the type of sign, we could have the following answers: we could have an accident that could injure another person or ourselves, we could lose our life, we might be fined, or even lose our license. Emphasize that traffic signs warn us about how we should drive on the roads, and if we don't follow them, we could have accidents, hurt someone, or be fined by the police.

Application: Just as authorities have set rules for how we should drive, God has also given rules through the Bible for how we should live. If we don't read, know, and follow them, we may harm others or ourselves, and in the end, face eternal death, which is the punishment for disobeying the rules. Read the suggested text.

Invitation: Invite the non-Christian children to receive Jesus so they can live according to God's will, and encourage those who are already converted to read the Bible every day.

Memory Verse: Genesis 9:13

2021

THE IRON

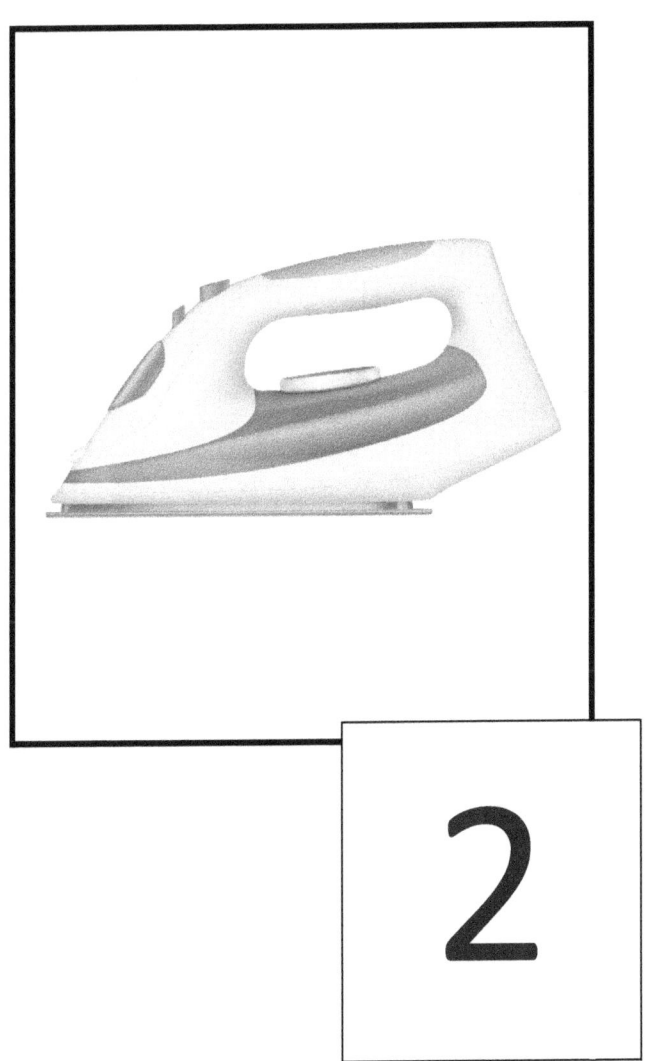

2

Object Lesson 2: The Iron

Materials: A household or toy iron.

Introduction: Ask the children what the object in their hands is used for. Then ask who has one at home. Emphasize that an iron is only used for clothes that are wrinkled (worn out); if the clothes aren't wrinkled, they don't need ironing. Ask the students: Who likes to go out with wrinkled, un-ironed clothes, either to the street or to an important event? If they are young children, explain that only an adult can use the iron and that it's dangerous. They should never use it without adult supervision.

Application: Just as we try to go out with our clothes ironed and wrinkle-free, God commands us to keep our spiritual garments, or our hearts, without stain or wrinkle. But these wrinkles can't be removed with an iron; only God can remove them. He is the only one who can see those wrinkles, and we cannot stand before Him like that.

Invitation: Invite the non-Christian children to receive Jesus so He can cleanse their hearts and forgive them. Encourage Christians to ask for forgiveness for their sins and turn away from them.

Memory Verse: Ephesians 5:27

2021

THE CELL PHONE

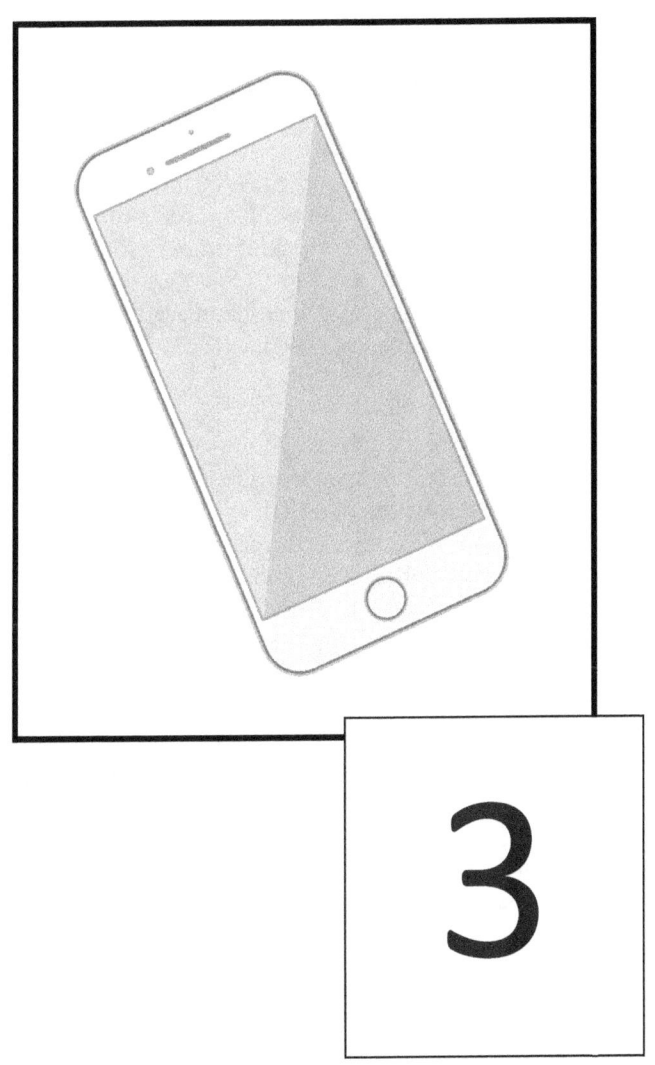

3

Object Lesson 3: The Cell Phone

Materials: A personal or toy cell phone.

Introduction: Who can explain to me what this object is used for? Who has one? The cell phone is a very important device for staying in touch with our families. Some people use it for work, and sometimes we use it to call for help from an institution like the police, fire department, ambulance, etc. (you can ask if anyone has done this). Also, emphasize that with this device, we can communicate over long distances, thanks to antennas and satellites. However, this device has some disadvantages, such as when there are natural disasters like earthquakes, storms, etc. The lines become overloaded or are cut off.

Application: Even though cell phones sometimes lose signal or the lines become overloaded, there is someone we can always talk to at any time, and He always listens to us. That someone is God! We don't need a cell phone; we simply need our hearts and our voices. Nothing can interrupt our communication with Him. You and I need to talk to God, whether we are happy or going through sad days. We should always talk to Him in prayer.

Invitation: Invite the non-Christian child to receive Jesus so they can be heard by God through prayer, and encourage the Christian child to continue praying.

Memory Verse: Jeremiah 33:3

2021

THE SOCCER BALL

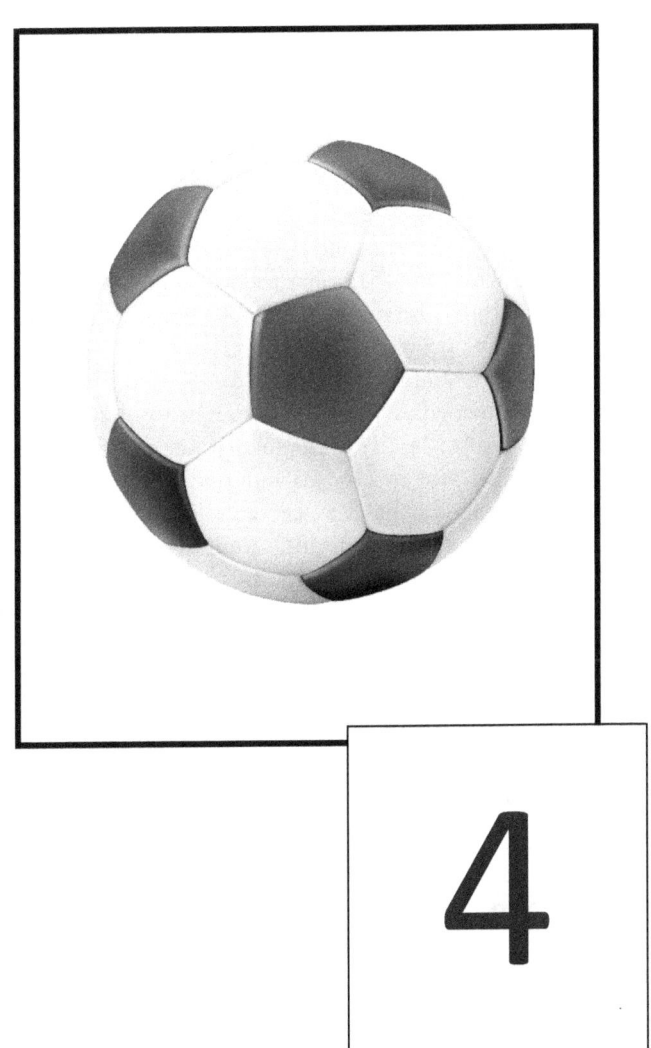

4

Object Lesson 4: The Soccer Ball.

Materials: A soccer ball.
Introduction: Hello, children! Can someone tell me what I brought today? The children respond, "a ball." How many of you like soccer? Who here can play? Who would like to play a soccer match? But today, we're not going to play. This ball brings us an important lesson. For those who like to play soccer, do you play by yourself? Or do you call your friends to make a team? Emphasize this point—that the ball is shared and that we play as a team, and that we usually look for friends to play with. This idea of finding friends to play with or share a toy or something else reminds me of a character in the Bible.

Application: It reminds me of the passage in John 1:35-42, where a man named Andrew, who sought to obey and serve God, and was also the first disciple of John, met the Messiah. John was a man sent by God to announce the coming of the Messiah (talk about the Messiah and His mission to save humanity from condemnation). Andrew, along with his teacher John, was waiting for the Messiah to come, and one day they found Him. John showed Andrew who He was, and when Andrew realized it, he immediately went to share the news with his brother Simon and brought him to Jesus without hesitation. Just like that, you and I should go to our friends and tell them about Jesus.

Invitation: Invite the non-Christian child and tell them that today they can meet Jesus by receiving Him. Encourage the Christian child to bring their friends next time.
Memory Verse: John 1:41

2021

THE LIFE JACKET

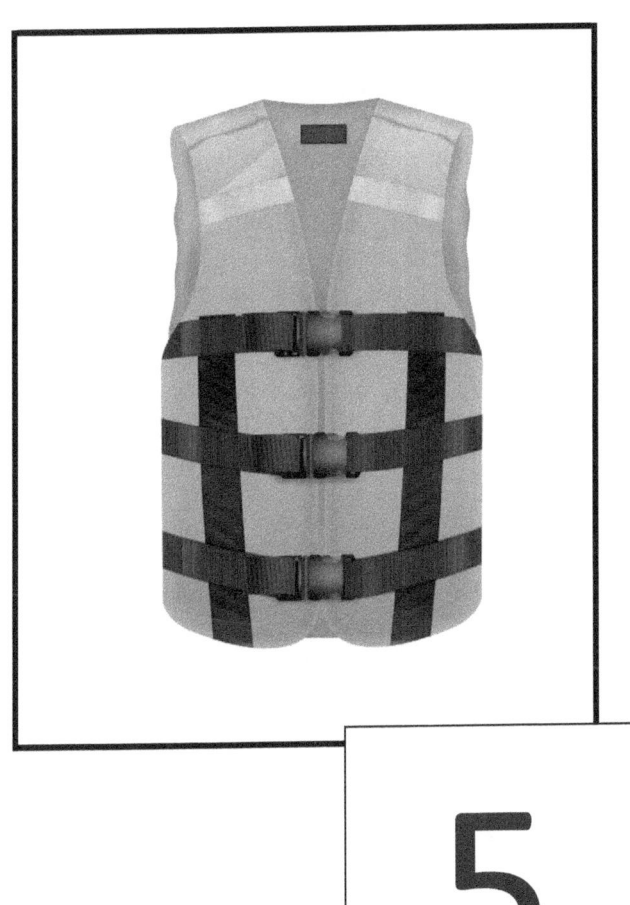

5

Object Lesson 5: The Life Jacket.

Materials: A life jacket.

Introduction: Hello, children! How are you? Who has been on a boat or a small vessel? Who knows how to swim? If someone doesn't know how to swim, what should they use if the boat sinks? The children should respond, "a life jacket." Today I brought a life jacket, which everyone who is on a boat should wear, especially if they don't know how to swim. Why do boats sink? The children might respond with answers like storms, collisions with other boats, rocks, icebergs, etc. Emphasize that in the sea, rivers, and lakes, there are many dangers, so all boats must have life jackets or emergency boats. If they don't, everyone will die, especially those who don't know how to swim. Stress that no other item can be used (you could mention Paul's shipwreck).

Application: This reminds me of a verse that tells us there is no other name or being in which we can be saved from the dangers we face in the world, such as our sin and evil. That name is Jesus! The verse is Acts 4:12, and it tells us that only Jesus can save us from the condemnation of our sins. Sin is the bad things we think, say, or do that do not please God. To be saved, we must turn to no one else, nothing else—only to Jesus. One day, we will stand before God to give an account, and if we've only done evil, we will be condemned. You can read Revelation 20:11-15.

Invitation: Invite the non-Christian child to receive Jesus to be saved from condemnation, and encourage the Christian child to stay firm in their faith.
Memory Verse: Acts 4:12

2021

THE AIRPLANE

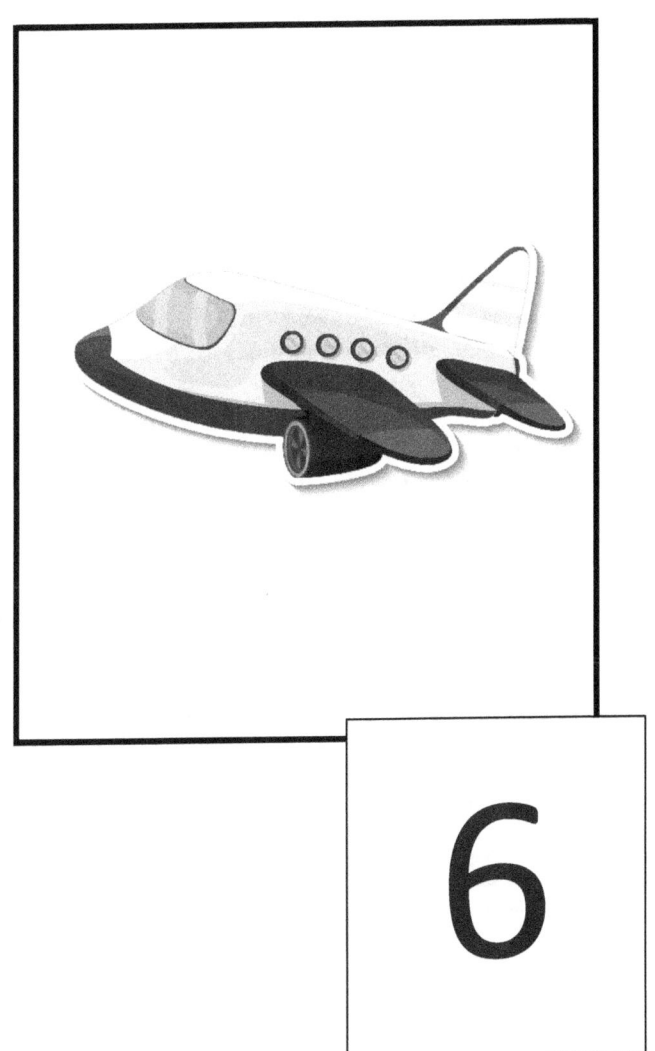

6

Object Lesson 6: The Airplane.

Materials: A toy airplane or a photograph of an airplane.
Introduction: Ask the children what you have in your hands. The children should respond, "a toy airplane." Who has flown on an airplane? Who would like to travel by airplane? The airplane is a great invention for humanity that took a lot of work to create. In ancient times, to travel long distances, people had to go by boat, walk, or ride horses, among other methods, which took a long time to reach the destination. Today, there are still places that can only be reached by airplane, small plane, or helicopter because vehicles cannot get there. By airplane, we can travel to the other side of the world and visit many countries. This reminds me of a command that the Lord Jesus gave us.

Application: The Lord commanded the first disciples to go into all the world, preaching the word of God and telling people that Jesus came to save them from their sins. This command is also for you and for me. We may not travel to other nations, but we can do it at home, in the neighborhood, in your town—wherever the Lord allows you to go, and according to the ability He has given you. We can read about this in Matthew 28:18-20. None of us can escape this command; we all must go and seek the lost.

Invitation: Invite the non-Christian child to receive Jesus and help them understand that Jesus has remembered them, allowing them to hear the message through the teacher. Encourage the Christian child to speak about Jesus to a friend or family member and bring them to the next class.
Memory Verse: Matthew 28:19

2021

THE MICROPHONE

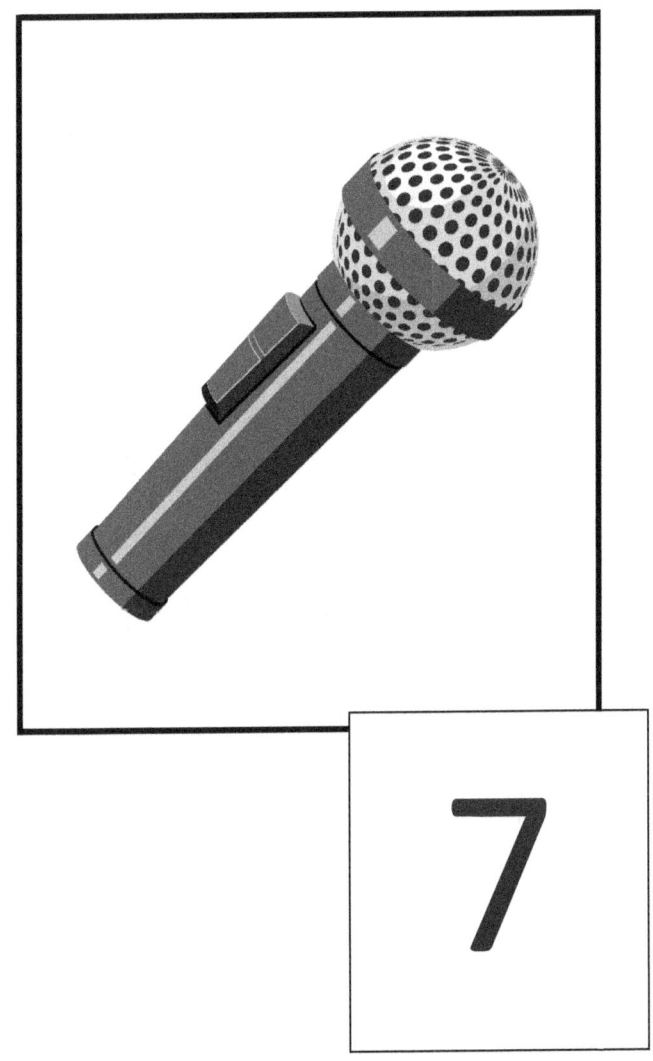

7

Object Lesson 7: The Microphone.

Materials: Bring a toy microphone or any microphone, preferably with an amplifier and speakers..

Introduction: Hello, children! Today I brought this object. Can anyone tell me what it is and what it's for? It converts sound into electrical signals, allowing us to transmit our words (or sounds) to a system that amplifies our voice so more people can hear us from a greater distance. If we only used our voice, our words would be heard over a shorter distance. Microphones are also found in cell phones and tablets, and they are used to record sounds or to speak with people who are far away.

Application: This object reminds me of a verse in the Bible, God's word, found in Proverbs, a book from the Old Testament, chapter 10, verse 19. Here, God tells us through Solomon (who wrote the book) that "in the multitude of words, sin is not lacking." This means that if we say everything we want or think, we could hurt others or ourselves, and sometimes we say bad things or use bad language, which offends God. This is called sin. Therefore, we must be careful with our words.

Invitation: Invite the non-Christian children to receive Christ to be forgiven for the wrong they have done against God. Encourage Christian children to ask forgiveness for the wrong things they have said and to stop doing it.

Memory Verse: Proverbs 10:19

2021

THE BOOK

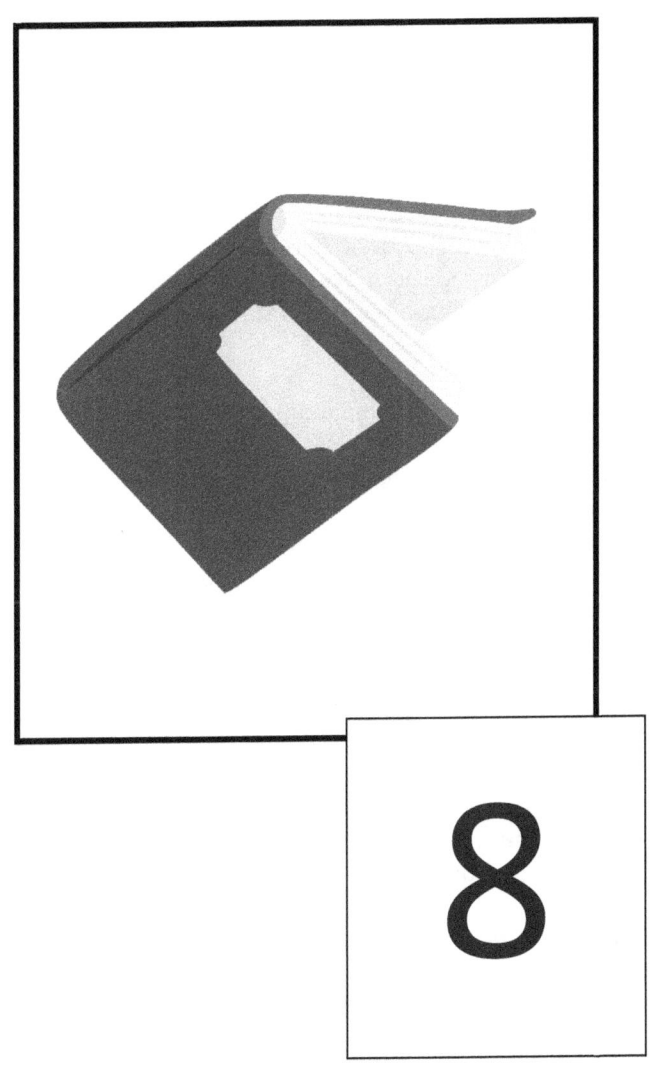

8

Object Lesson 8: The Book.

Materials: Bring any book or a phone directory.

Introduction: Who likes to read? Do you have a favorite book apart from the Bible? Is there any author you admire? Today, I brought a book of poems by a famous poet. In the world, there are many books on all kinds of topics, and to read them all, it would take hundreds or thousands of years. Nations have always had places called libraries where they store many books with all kinds of information to preserve it for the future, such as books on mathematics, Spanish, history, etc. Today, digital media like computers are used to store thousands or millions of books in a small space.

Application: This book reminds me of some books that John saw in the book of Revelation. There were books where everything we do in this world is written down—things that you and I do, whether they are good or bad. All of this will be revealed at the end of time, during God's judgment on mankind. But there will be a special book called the Book of Life, where the names of those who will be saved are written, and they will live with God forever. Those whose names are not written will be thrown into the lake of fire (you can read Revelation 20:12-15 and Luke 10:20).

Invitation: Invite the non-Christian children to receive Christ, so their names will be written in the Book of Life. Encourage the Christian children to thank God that their names are written in the Book of Life.

Memory Verse: Revelation 20:15

2021

THE GLASSES

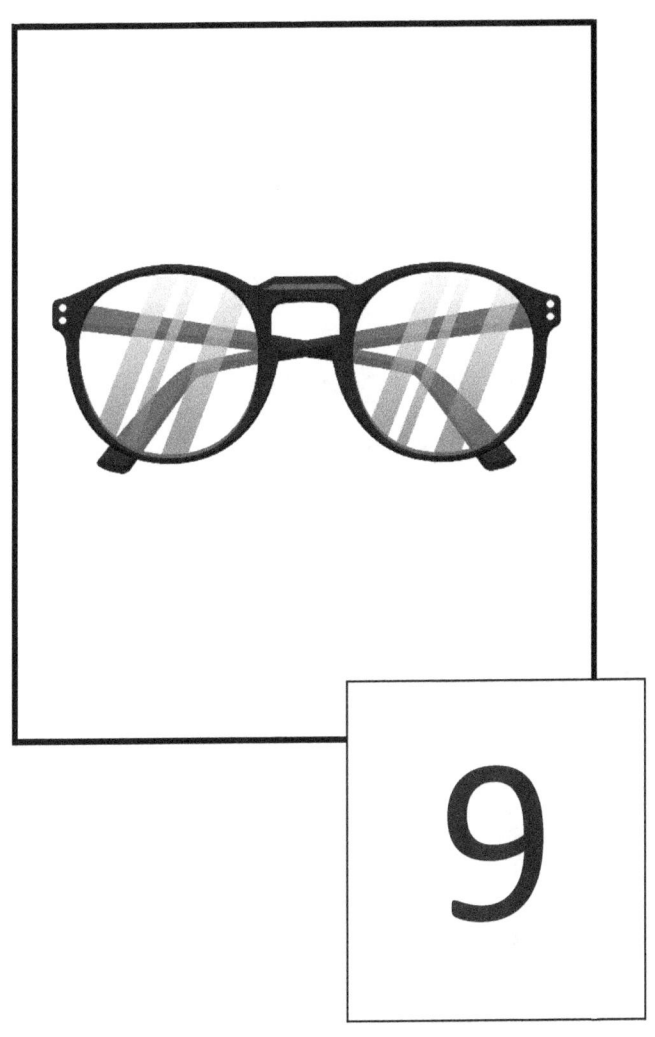

9

Object Lesson 9: Glasses.

Materials: Bring personal glasses, either used or toy glasses.

Introduction: Hello, children! Today, I've brought this object. Does anyone know what it's called? What is it for? Many people around the world use it to see better, or maybe just to read. Some people wear glasses to protect their eyes from computers or electronic devices, or to protect themselves from the sun. What would happen if we took the glasses away from someone who has trouble seeing? Maybe they couldn't see far or close, maybe they wouldn't be able to read, or they couldn't walk freely because they would be afraid of stumbling.

Application: These glasses remind me of a commandment that God gave us, which is written in Proverbs 23:26, where the Lord asks us to let our eyes look straight ahead, following His ways. This means that we should do what is right in God's eyes, staying away from bad things, being careful not to do evil or look at bad things, especially on TV and the internet, through cell phones and tablets. If you're watching TV or using the internet and suddenly something that doesn't please God appears, you should change the channel or close the program and look for something that pleases God. Reading the Bible helps us know what is good and what is bad, so we don't stumble.

Invitation: Invite the non-Christian child to receive Jesus so they can be saved, and the Lord will help them stay away from what is bad. Encourage the Christian child to avoid doing things that displease God, and not to sin.
Memory Verse: Proverbs 23:26

2021

SPORTS SHOES

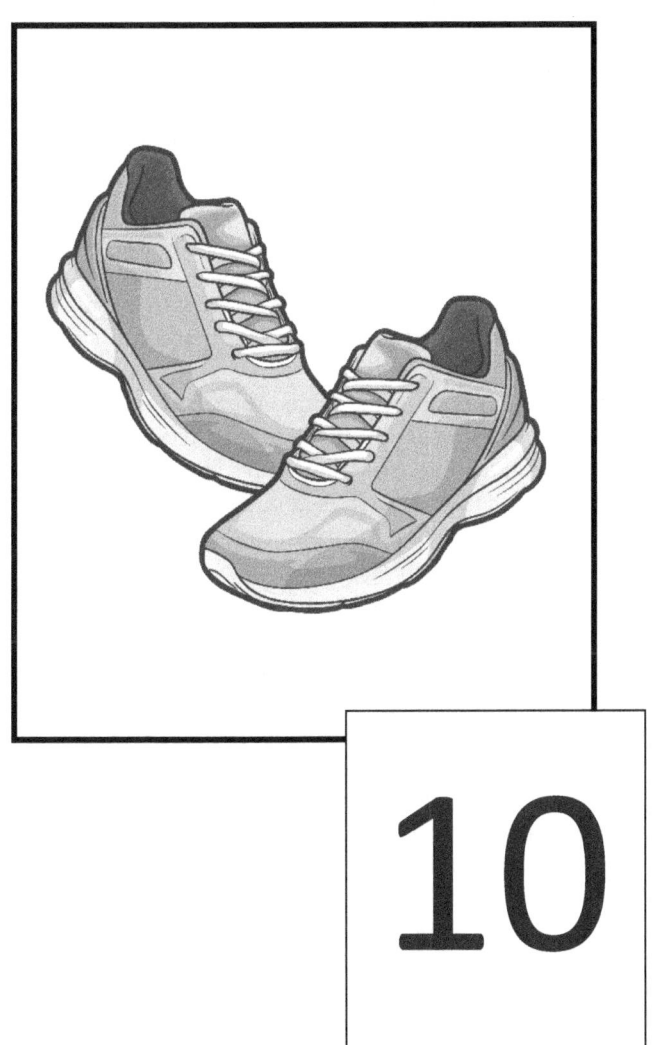

10

Object Lesson 10: Sports Shoes.

Material: A pair of sports shoes.

Introduction: Hello, children! Today I've brought some shoes, but they are not just any shoes. Can anyone tell me what activity we can use them for? (Children should respond that they are for sports.) That's right! With these shoes, we can play sports, such as running, jumping, riding a bicycle, etc. You can't run in boots or regular shoes because they could damage the shoes and even hurt our feet and knees. So, it's not recommended to do sports with the wrong shoes. With good sports shoes, you can run for miles, and if you're fast, you can win competitions and earn prizes. In races, the winner is the one who finishes first, and to get there, you must train a lot (emphasize this point).

Application: These shoes remind me of a Bible verse where the Apostle Paul encourages us to run a race, but it's not just any race, and it's not about sports. It's about the race of faith. What does that mean? It means that all of us who have received Jesus in our hearts must keep going every day, believing in Jesus Christ, and also exercising ourselves. How? By reading the Bible, praying, and gathering in church. That way, we can be prepared to obey and serve Him, not stopping halfway, but continuing until the day He comes or we pass away physically, and then we will be rewarded by being in His presence. (Acts 20:24)

Invitation: Encourage Christian children to keep going and pray for them; motivate them to pray, read the Bible, and attend church. Invite non-Christian children to receive Jesus to start the race and receive the reward of eternal life.

Memory Verse: 2 Timothy 4:7

2021

THE HEADPHONES

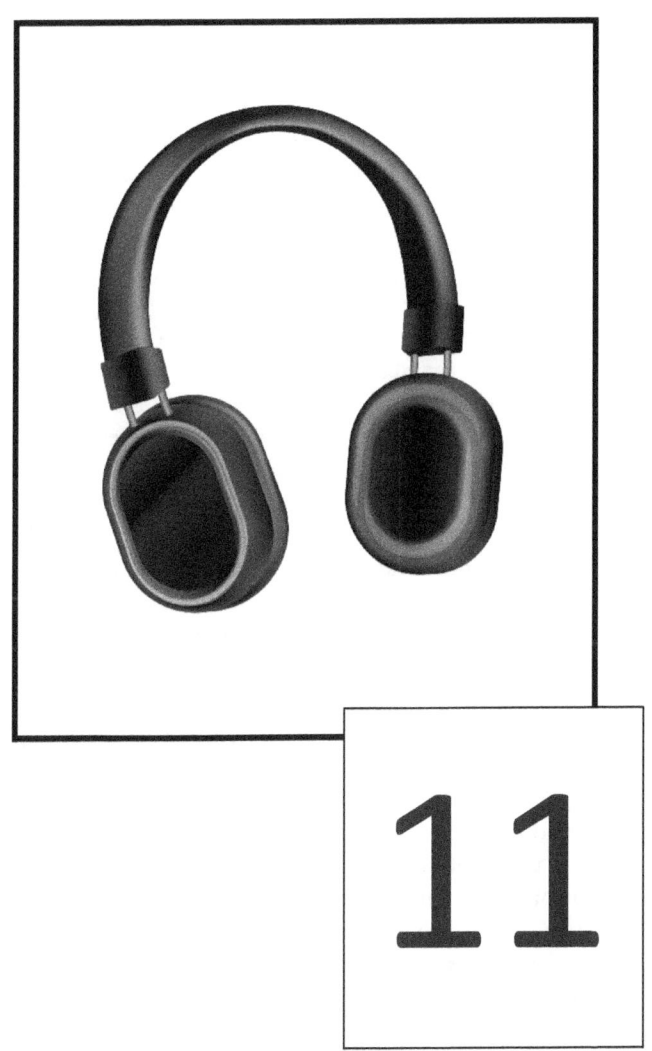

11

Object Lesson 11: Headphones.

Material: A pair of headphones.

Introduction: Good afternoon, children! Today I brought a very well-known object. Can anyone tell me what it is called? That's right! It's a pair of headphones. What is it used for? (Children should respond that it is used to listen to music, videos, etc.) As you said, headphones help us connect to devices like cell phones, tablets, computers, televisions, and others, so we can clearly hear what they are playing (it could be music or videos). Using headphones allows us to listen to the audio privately without interrupting others. Sometimes we also use them because the device volume is too low, and there might be a lot of noise around us. What kind of music do you listen to? What videos do you watch or have you seen?

Application: These headphones remind me of a verse in the Bible, which is in Romans 10:17 (read the verse). This verse tells us that faith in God comes after hearing messages about Him or Jesus Christ. What is faith in God or in His Word? It means that you and I believe that Jesus is the Savior of the world, and that whoever believes in Him and obeys Him is saved from eternal condemnation. If you have not believed in Jesus and do not obey Him, you can do so today because God has given you the opportunity to hear the message. And if you already believe in Jesus, you must listen to His Word every day. How? By reading the Bible, listening to sermons, going to church, or even listening to the Bible in audio (because now you can listen to it in MP3 or videos). You should not listen to other things that can draw you away from faith and God's commandments (examples: videos or music that do not worship and exalt God).

Invitation: Ask if anyone wants to accept Christ, and ask Christian children to stop listening to wrong things and to ask for forgiveness if they have been doing so.

Memory verse: Romans 10:17

2021

THE TABLET

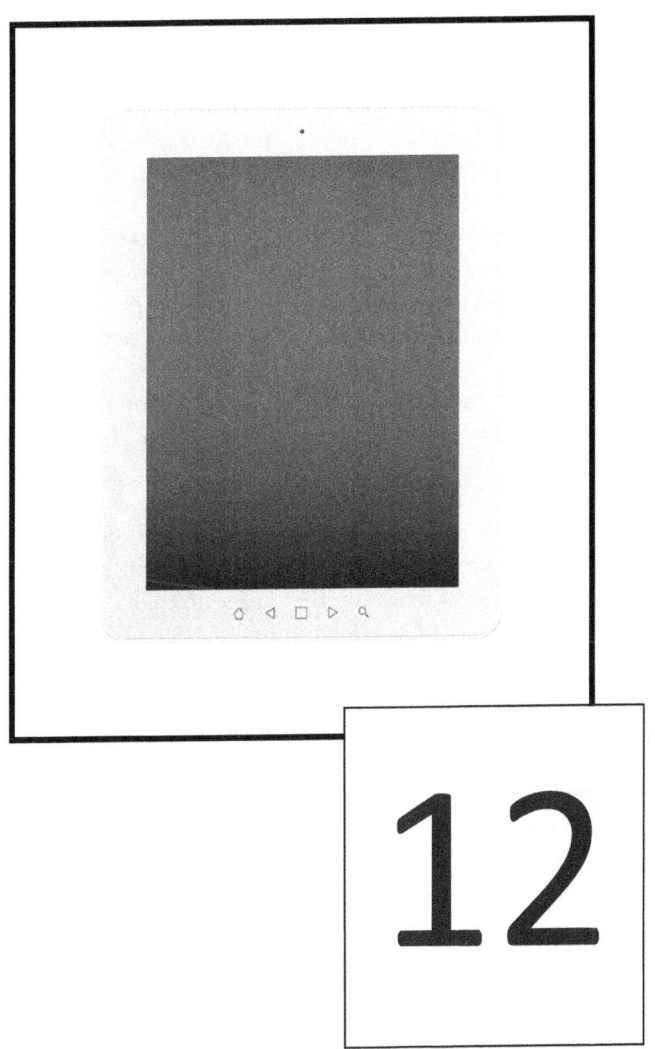

12

Object Lesson 12: The Tablet.

Materials: A real or toy tablet.

Introduction:
Teacher: "Hello, children! Today I have brought this device. What is it called? What can we do with a tablet?"
Children: "It's a tablet! With tablets, we can watch videos, browse the internet, and use social media like Facebook, Twitter, etc."
Teacher: "That's right, children! With tablets, we can do many things, such as browsing the internet and using social media, talking to our friends and family, and even to people we don't personally know. We can also watch videos, listen to audio, and more. But some things on social media can be bad, and sometimes we might fall into the trap of saying wrong things to others. This reminds me of a verse from 1 Corinthians 15:33."

Application: This verse tells us that bad conversations corrupt good habits. In other words, we can say that bad company can lead us down the wrong path. That's why you should be careful (if you have Jesus in your heart) with who you spend your time with, whether at school, in your neighborhood, or especially on social media. If you hang out with foolish people, you'll suffer harm.

Invitation: Encourage the Christian child to choose their friends wisely, and invite non-believers to receive Christ and stop doing wrong to avoid condemnation.
Memory Verse: 1 Corinthians 15:33

THE TIE

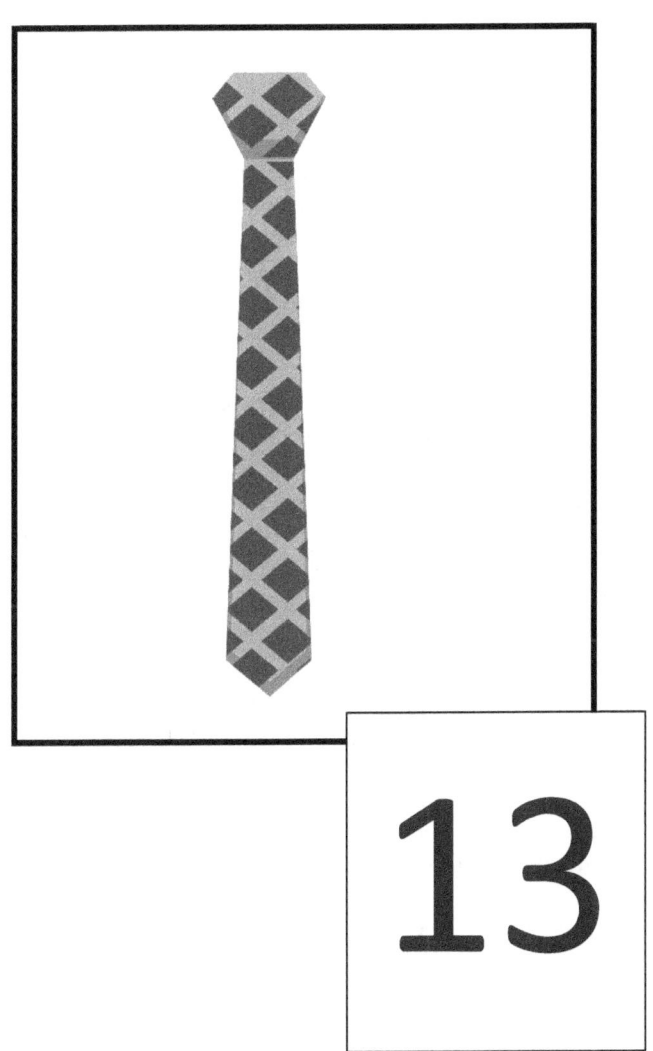

Object Lesson 13: The Tie.

Materials: Any tie.

Introduction: Hello kids! Who can tell me what this is called? That's right! It's a tie! When do we wear a tie? To go to the park? No, we wear a tie for special or important events. Can you tell me what kind of events? Correct! We wear ties for activities like meetings, work, weddings, birthdays, and more. Has anyone of you worn a tie? Do you know anyone who wears a tie? (Wait for the children's responses.) Now, let's do a demonstration of how to wear a tie. Is there any volunteer? (Invite one or more children to try on the tie.) As we mentioned, ties are worn for important events like a wedding. Has anyone ever been to a wedding?

Application: All this talk about ties reminds me of a passage in the Bible that talks about a wedding, called the "wedding of the Lamb" in Revelation 19:7. The text tells us that Jesus will be the groom, and all those who believe in Him and follow God's commandments will be the bride. If you have believed in Jesus and received Him, you can be sure you will be there. But if you haven't, sadly, you won't be able to attend. The Bible teaches that the church is the bride of the Lamb, who is Christ, and she must present herself to Him pure and spotless (2 Corinthians 11:2)—in other words, without sin. And the only way to be presented spotless is by accepting Christ as our Savior; only He can cleanse us.

Invitation: To the unconverted children, encourage them to receive Christ to be cleansed; and to the converted ones, encourage them to remain firm, waiting for the moment when we will be before the Lord.

Memory Verse: Revelation 19:7

2021

THE CALENDAR

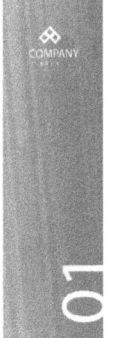

Object Lesson 14: The Calendar.

Materials: A calendar.

Introduction: Today, I brought this object. Can anyone tell me what it's called? That's right! It's a calendar. What is a calendar for? (Wait for children's responses.) A calendar shows us the months of the year, the weeks in each month, and the days of the week. Can anyone tell me what important dates this calendar reminds you of? (Listen to responses.) For me, it reminds me of several dates like my birthday, Mother's Day, Father's Day, Christmas, Independence Day—these dates never change on the calendar, so we know exactly when they will be or how many days are left until that date. This helps us get ready to make purchases or avoid making other commitments.

Application: This calendar reminds me of a passage in the Bible, Matthew 24:36-51 (read it aloud). The text talks about the coming of the Lord Jesus, when He will come for His church to take it to heaven, to the wedding of the Lamb, and to save us from the coming judgment that will come upon the whole world. But the day He will come, no one knows—it's a date that doesn't appear on any calendar! So, if you have received Jesus in your heart, you must try to do good every day. And if you haven't received Jesus into your heart, today is the day you can do so, so that when He comes, He will come for you, and you won't be condemned or have to face God's judgment.

Invitation: Encourage the converted children not to get discouraged by any mockery they might face for waiting for Jesus, and urge the unconverted children to avoid judgment and not delay their decision to receive Jesus.

Memory Verse: Matthew 24:36

2021

THE FRUITS

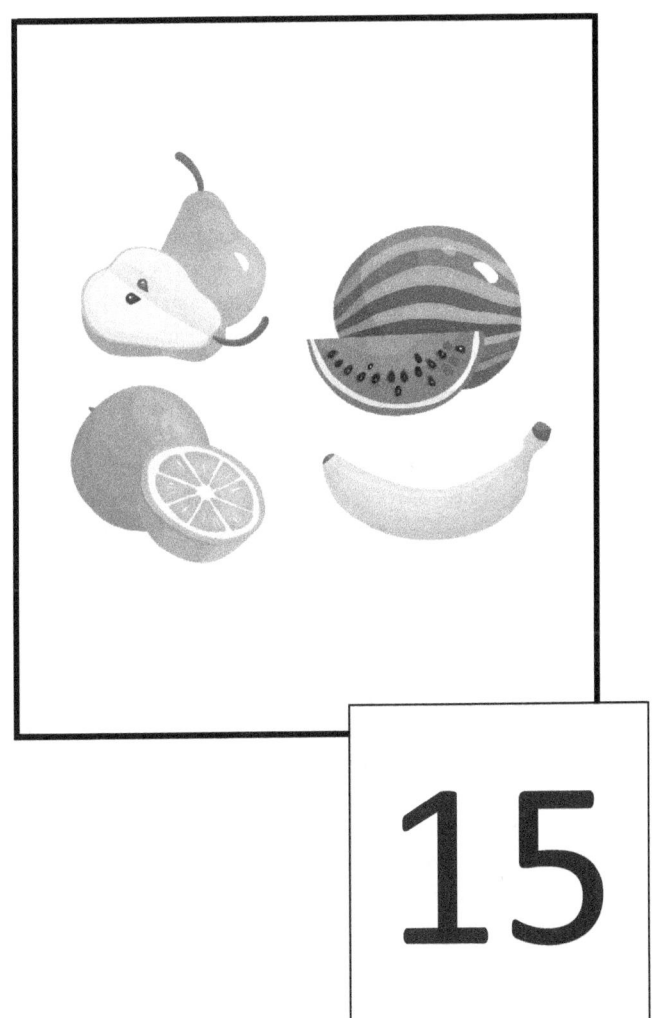

15

Object Lesson 15: The Fruits.

Materials: Various fruits.

Introduction: Hello, kids! How have you been? Can anyone tell me what these things are called that I brought? That's right! Today, I brought these fruits (mention the fruits you brought), and they are very delicious. Who here likes fruit? (If possible, give a piece of fruit to each child and let them try it.) Not only are they delicious, but they are also important for our health. It's always good to eat fruit. But for us to eat them, they need to be in good condition—that is, clean and ripe. They shouldn't be rotten. What happens if we eat a rotten fruit? We can get sick! Do you think an orange tree can produce mangoes? No! Every tree produces fruit according to its type.

Application: All this talk about fruit reminds me of a Bible verse in Galatians 5:22-26 that talks about the "fruit" of the Spirit (read the passage). The text tells us that the fruit of the Spirit is: love, joy, peace, patience, kindness, goodness, gentleness, and self-control. (Explain the meaning of each word to the children.) This means that if you have received Jesus in your heart, all these things should be visible in your life. Otherwise, you need to sincerely receive Jesus so that the Holy Spirit can renew your heart, or you need to strive to do what is good and ask God to help you. Remember, an orange tree can't produce mangoes, and likewise, a child of God can't keep doing what is wrong. If you keep doing wrong things, it may be that you're not really a child of God (give examples of bad fruit, such as hatred, fighting, etc.).

Invitation: If you have already received Jesus, you should strive to show the fruit of the Spirit or ask the Lord for strength. If you haven't received Jesus yet, today you can do so, so that God's love and joy can be manifested in you and you can receive salvation.

Memory Verse: Galatians 5:22

2021

THE TREE

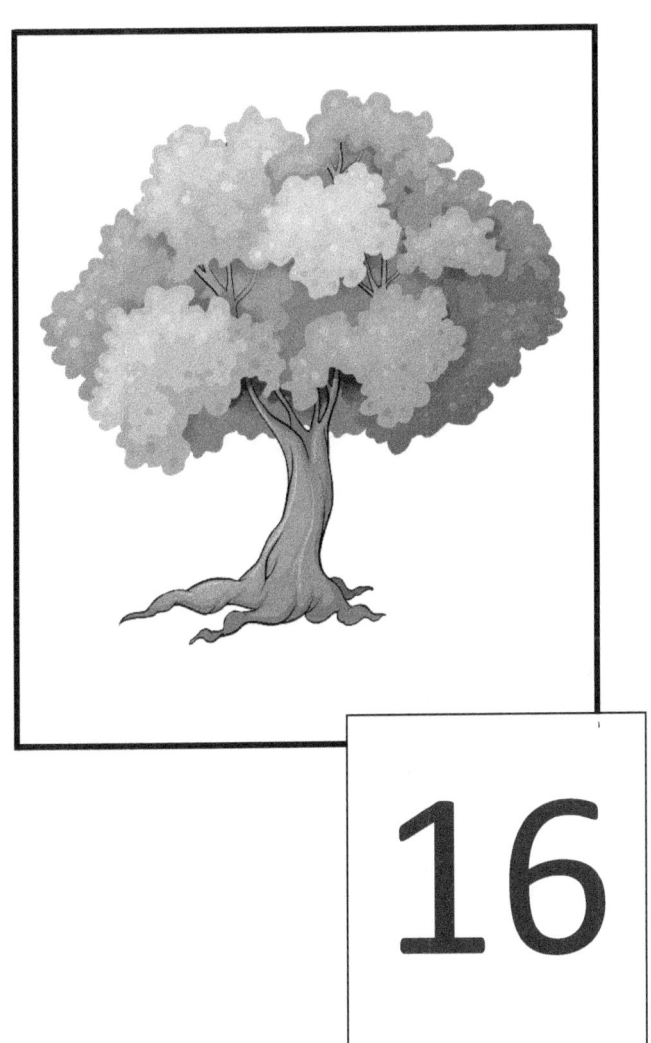

16

Object Lesson 16: The Tree.

Material: A small fruit tree (e.g., mango).

Introduction: Hello kids! Today, I've brought this little tree. Can anyone tell me what type of tree it is? What is the fruit it produces? (Listen to answers.) This little tree I brought is a mango tree. Right now, it's too young to produce mangos; it will take many years. Normally, a tree produces fruit around 5 years after the seed has sprouted. Do you think mangoes are good fruit or bad? Mangoes are good fruit! They contain lots of vitamins that help your body. Do you know of any fruit that is bad? (Give examples.) Some trees produce fruit that is poisonous or substances that can harm us; therefore, they can't be eaten. All of this reminds me of a Bible passage from the Book of Matthew 7:17.

Application: This passage is found in the book of Matthew, which is part of the New Testament, in chapter 7, verses 17 through 20 (read the text). This passage tells us that good trees bear good fruit, and bad trees bear bad fruit. However, it's not really talking about trees in the field, since all trees have a purpose. Instead, it's talking about people. If you say you are a child of God and have accepted Jesus into your heart, you cannot do bad things (give examples: saying bad words, stealing, killing, watching inappropriate things online, having bad friendships, etc.). If you do bad things, you are bad, and therefore, you are not a child of God. If you are a good tree, you should produce good fruit (give examples: love, respect, fear of God, obedience to parents, praying, reading the Bible, etc.).

Invitation: If you are a Christian child who has accepted Jesus, you must produce good fruit.

Memory Verse: Matthew 7:17

September 2021

THE CHAIR

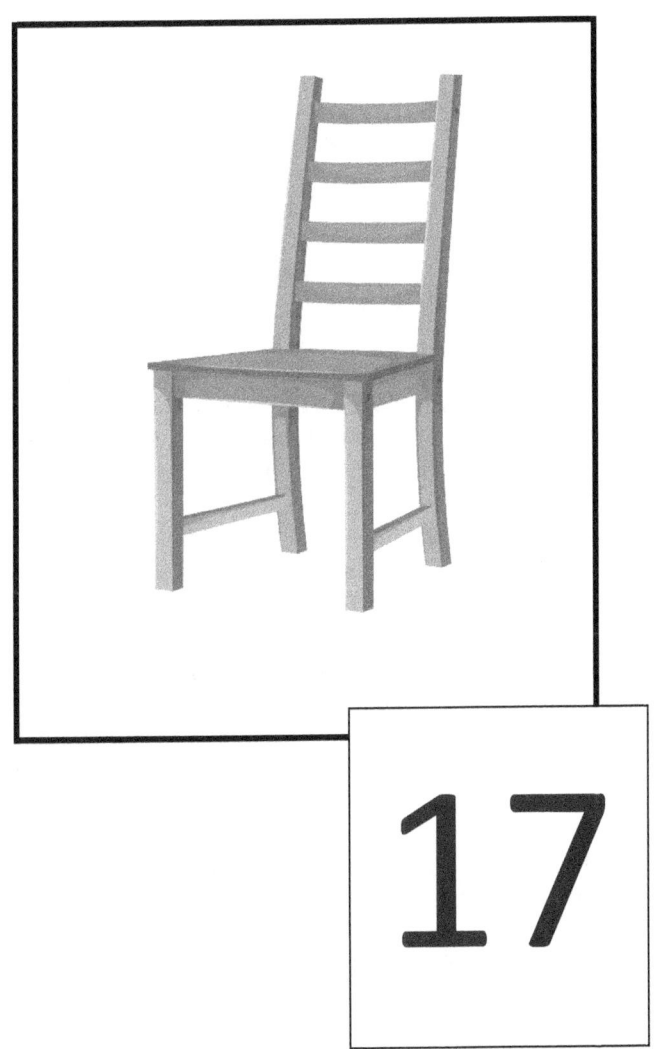

17

Object Lesson 17: The Chair.

Material: A chair of any type.

Introduction: Can anyone tell me what this object is called? That's right! It's a chair! Can someone tell me what it's used for? (Listen to responses.) Chairs are used for sitting. Why do we sit on chairs? (Listen to responses.) Chairs are useful for many activities we do, like eating, studying, watching TV, resting, and one day, when we grow up, we'll use them in the office to work. Almost every home and company uses chairs. Are all chairs the same? That's right! There are many types of chairs: dining chairs, recliners, office chairs, plastic chairs, and wooden chairs. Even in courtrooms, where prisoners are taken, there's a judge who sits on a chair and decides whether a person is guilty or innocent of the charges against them.

Application: All this talk about chairs and judges reminds me of a passage in Revelation 20:11-15 (read the text). This passage speaks about a great white throne. Does anyone know what a throne is? A throne is a special type of chair where kings sit. The Bible tells us there was a great white throne, and someone was sitting on it—that was God! Before Him stood all who had died, and they were judged there. Everyone in the world will be there, whether they believed in God or not, and they will have to give an account to Him for everything they've done. If you've accepted Christ and follow His commandments, you won't have to stand before that throne. But if you've never accepted Christ and live according to your own ways, doing what's wrong, then yes, you will be there!

Invitation: If the child is already a believer, encourage them to thank God for His forgiveness and salvation and to remain steadfast. If the child is not yet a believer, encourage them to trust in Christ and stop doing wrong so they won't face condemnation.

Memory Verse: Revelation 20:11

September 2021

THE BILL

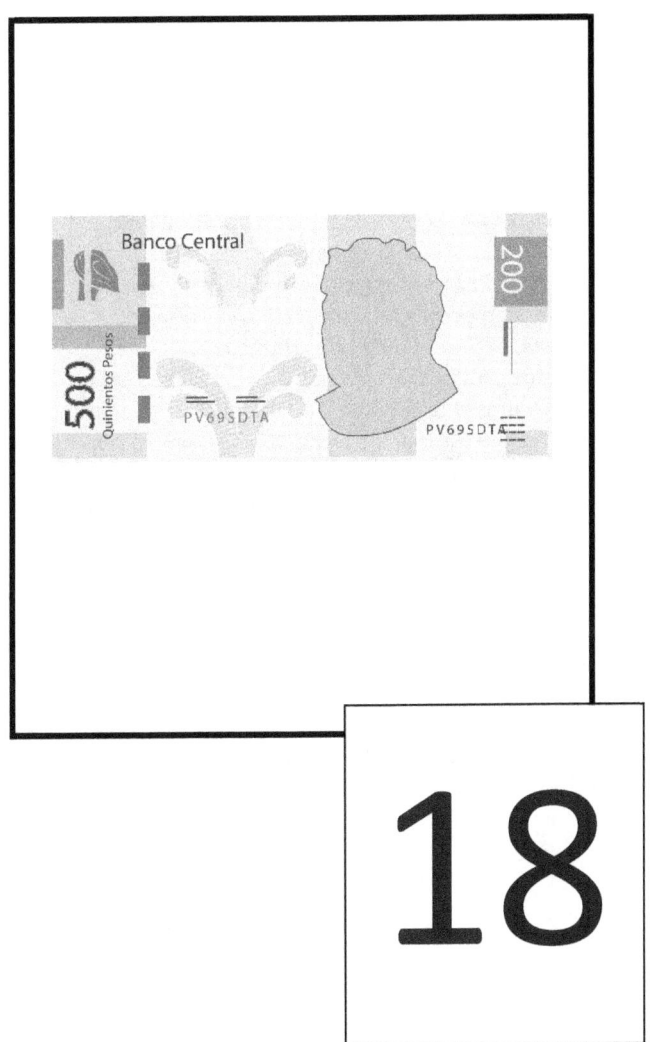

Object Lesson 18: The Bill.

Material: A bill (with the highest denomination possible).

Introduction: Can anyone tell me what this is that I've brought today? That's right! It's a hundred-dollar bill. Who here would like to have lots of bills like this one? What would you buy? (Listen to answers.) Everyone likes to have money to do many things, like buying cars, houses, phones, land, traveling, or hiring employees—the list goes on. Some people use it for good things, while others use it for bad things. Do you think having a lot of money makes us better people? (Listen to responses.) The truth is, no. Maybe you know people who have millions or billions of dollars, but they're bad people. Some think that if we love God, we must have lots of money, but that's not always true. If it were, then many rich people who are very wicked would have Jesus in their hearts, or God would be with them.

Application: All of this reminds me of a Bible passage in Psalm 73:1-17. Psalms is in the Old Testament (read the passage). This text talks about Asaph, who was a psalmist. He felt envious of wicked people who had lots of money and seemed to gain more every day. Asaph saw how they mistreated others, didn't work hard, and even spoke against God. Seeing all of this made Asaph feel discouraged because he walked the straight path, loved God, and served Him, yet he felt he faced more problems than they did. But one day, Asaph realized he shouldn't envy them because their end would be disastrous. Suddenly, they would face sorrow and pain, and in the end, they would be condemned.

Invitation: Encourage the Christian child not to envy wicked people but to feel grateful to God for salvation. Encourage the non-Christian child not to trust in money or worldly things but to trust in Christ and receive Him as their Savior to have eternal life and salvation.

Memory Verse: Psalm 73:2-3

September 2021

BALD BOY BABY DOLL

19

Object Lesson 19: Bald boy baby doll.

Material: Bald boy baby doll (large doll).

Introduction: Hello kids! How have you been? Can anyone tell me what this is that I've brought today? That's right! It's a boy baby doll, and some people call it a Bald boy baby doll. This doll represents a tiny baby, just after being born. Before babies are born, they grow inside their mommy's tummy—they're not brought by a stork like people used to say. All of us were once small, helpless babies who needed the protection of our moms and dads. Many moms and dads are thrilled when they find out they'll have a baby. However, some parents don't feel happy—they feel sad because they think having a baby will ruin their life or future. On the other hand, many men and women cry because they can't have a baby, even though they deeply desire one. Some turn to doctors for help; sometimes it works, but other times it doesn't.

Application: All of this reminds me of a Bible verse in Psalm 127:3 (read the verse). This verse says that children are a gift from God, a reward for their parents, especially if the parents love God. So, when you and I were born, we were a gift from God to our parents—even if they didn't see it that way or felt sad about it. Every baby is a miracle growing inside a woman's womb. Babies are a gift, but sometimes this world and Satan make us believe that babies are a burden or unnecessary. Some mothers are even encouraged to kill their baby while it's still in the womb. But you and I need to understand that babies are a gift from God.

Invitation: If you've accepted Jesus, you should be thankful to God for allowing you to be born and for making you a gift. And even more now that He has saved you from eternal death! If you haven't accepted Christ yet, you can do so today to receive eternal life.

Memory Verse: Psalm 127:3

September 20, 2021

THE TRUMPET

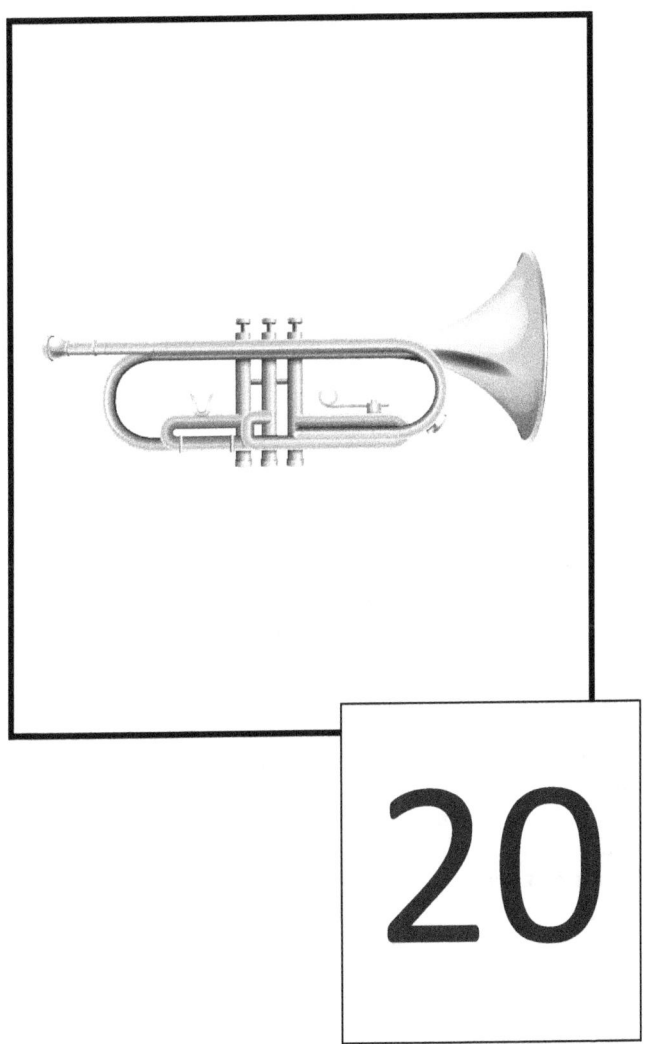

20

Object Lesson 20: The Trumpet.

Material: A trumpet (real or toy).

Introduction: God bless you, children! Today, I have brought this object. What is it called? That's right! It's a trumpet! The trumpet is a musical instrument that has existed for many years (you can demonstrate the sound or let a child try playing the trumpet). In ancient times, the trumpet was used for different activities, such as music, religious ceremonies in temples, hunting, and more. It was also used in war to signal orders to warriors, such as advancing, retreating, or other commands, depending on the sound. Therefore, soldiers or warriors had to pay close attention to the orders given through the trumpet and learn what each sound meant. (Mention that trumpets have been very famous because they are simple and portable wind instruments.)

Application: This reminds me of a passage in 1 Corinthians 15:51 (read the passage). This verse talks about a future event when a trumpet will be blown by an angel of God to announce an important event we call the Rapture of the Church. That trumpet will announce that those who have died in Christ will be resurrected, and those who are alive will be transformed. This special event does not have a set date; we don't know when it will happen, but it will be very special for those of us who believe in Christ. That's why we should be thankful to the Lord and strive to serve Him with all our hearts while we wait for that day. It doesn't matter whether we are alive or have physically died; that day will come, and the Lord will take us to the marriage supper of the Lamb, where we will be rewarded according to our works.

Invitation: If you are a Christian, give thanks to God for your salvation; and if you have not yet received Jesus, today you can do so to ensure that you are taken in the Rapture and won't remain to face God's judgments.

Memory Verse: 1 Corinthians 15:51

September 20, 2021

THE CROSS

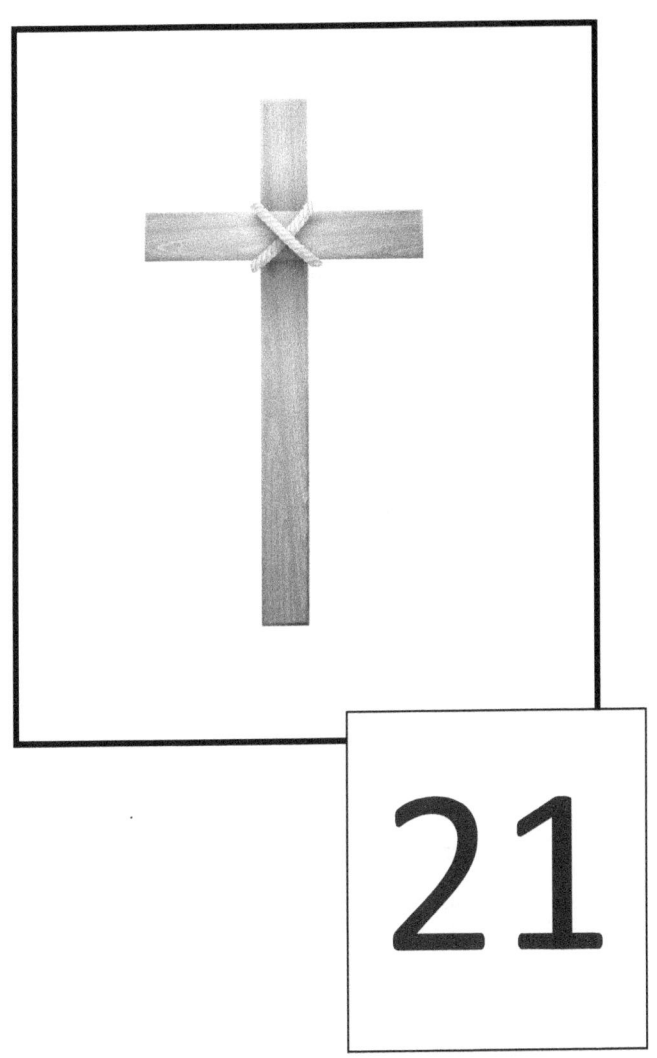

Object Lesson 21: The Cross.

Material: A cross (made of any material).

Introduction: Hello, children! God bless you! Today, I have brought this object. Can anyone tell me what it's called? That's right! It's a cross! The cross is a symbol known all around the world, and it generally represents the Christian religion. Within Christianity, there are many groups of churches, such as Catholics, Evangelicals, Lutherans, Anglicans, and others. Although the cross now represents a religion, thousands of years ago, it didn't symbolize anything religious. Instead, the cross was a symbol of punishment. Many people condemned to death were nailed to a cross as punishment for their wrongdoings or because they were prisoners of war. Crosses were built in different shapes: like a "T," like an "X," like a "Y," or as we know it today, like a plus sign but with a longer vertical line (†). Other times, it was just a single post, like an "I." A person nailed to a cross could sometimes take days or hours to die. Before being crucified, they were often whipped and treated very poorly. No one would want to die in such a way!

Application: All this about the cross reminds me of a Bible verse in 1 Corinthians 1:18. This verse says that some people see the sacrifice or death of Jesus on the cross as foolishness or something unimportant. If we had lived in those times, we would probably think that only criminals and bad people died on the cross. But for us who believe in Christ and have received Him, we know that Jesus' death on the cross means our salvation and the forgiveness of sins (sins are the bad things we do, say, or think that displease God). Jesus' death on the cross represents the punishment for our sins, as before God, we are all sinners. Jesus symbolically carried those sins on His shoulders, sparing you and me from eternal punishment. Through this, we were forgiven and saved.

Invitation: Encourage non-believing children to accept Jesus to be forgiven and receive eternal life. Motivate believing children to share the message of Christ's sacrifice with others.

Memory Verse: 1 Corinthians 1:18

September 20, 2021

WATER, ICE, AND VAPOR

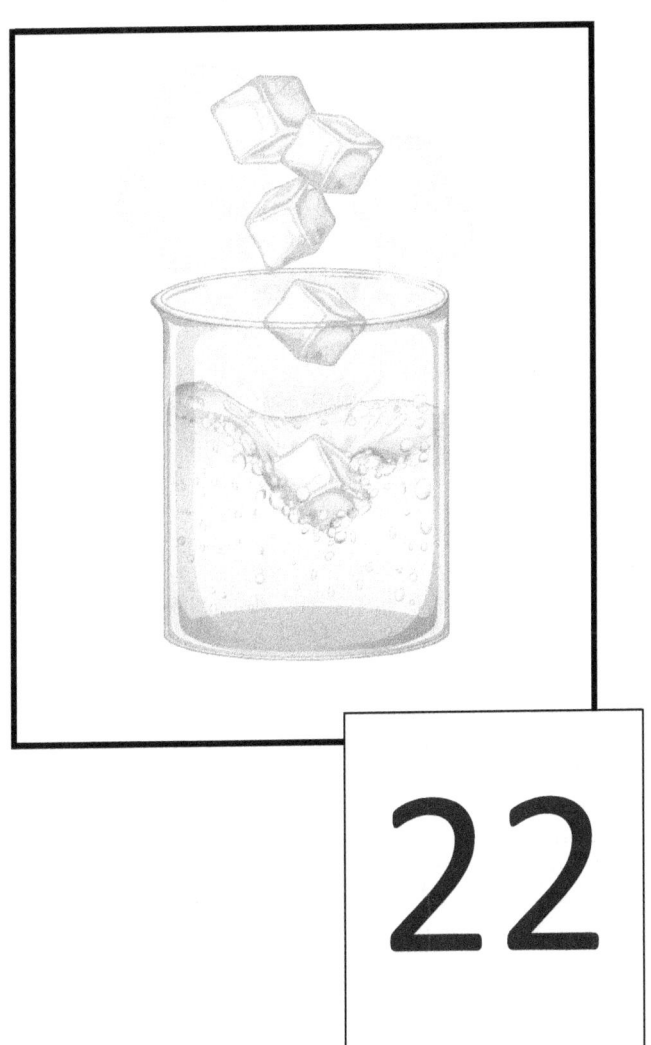

22

Object Lesson 22: Water, Ice, and Vapor.

Material: Water, ice, and vapor (for vapor, you can use an empty bottle). You can also bring photos or images.

Introduction: Hello, children! Today, I've brought these containers with something inside. Can you tell me what it is? That's right! Water, ice, and in this bottle, we'll imagine there is water vapor. In school, we learn that water has three states: liquid, solid, and gas. At normal temperature, water is liquid; when it freezes, it becomes solid, and when it is heated, it evaporates. When water turns into vapor in small amounts, we can't see it, but in large quantities, it appears as clouds. Water is incredible because of its unique properties. It is essential for life on Earth, and when water is absent in some parts of the world, life disappears, leaving only sand, dirt, and dust. (Regardless of the state we find water in, it doesn't lose its properties; it always remains H_2O.)

Application: This condition of water and its importance reminds me of a Bible verse where God reveals Himself in three distinct persons, even though He is one God. This is something we cannot fully understand, and no human being can explain it completely. One of these verses is in Luke 3:21-22 (read the passage). Here we see Jesus, the Holy Spirit (who descends from heaven), and God (speaking from heaven) all appearing at the same time. We consider all three as God, with the power to forgive sins and grant salvation. Let's also read John 10:30-33, where Jesus clearly states that He is one with the Father. We may not fully comprehend all these things, but one thing is clear: if God is not present in a person's life, their life becomes like death, like a desert.

Invitation: Encourage the non-believing child to receive Christ, to gain eternal life and avoid walking in the desert of sadness, pain, and condemnation. Motivate the believing child to share Christ with others and to understand the importance of God in our lives.

Memory Verse: John 10:30

September 20, 2021

THE WIG

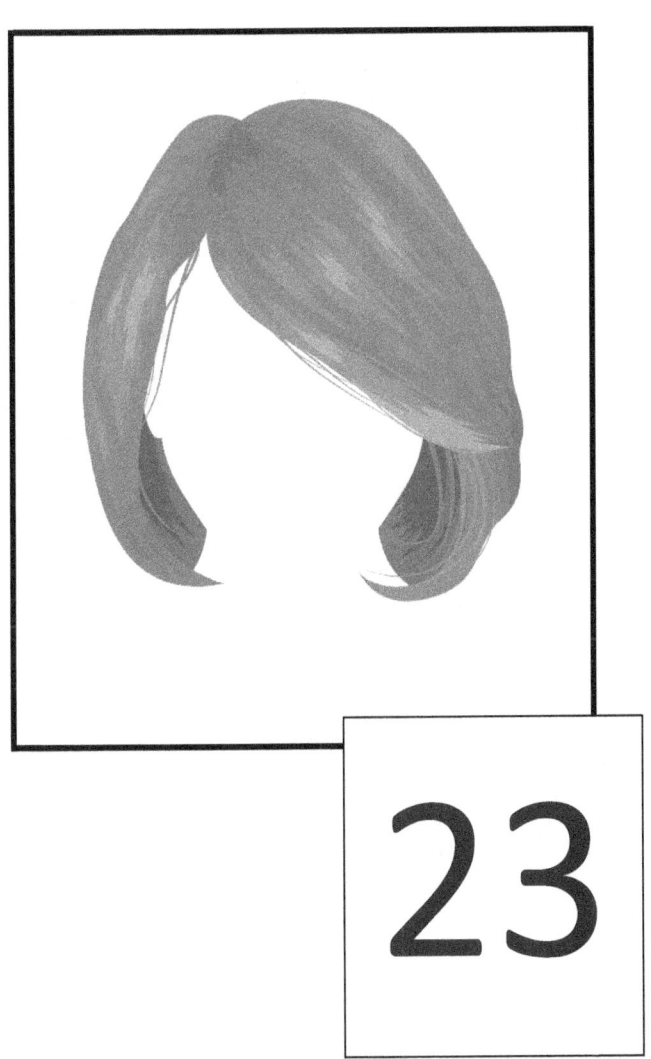

23

Object Lesson 23: The Wig.

Material: A wig.

Introduction: Hello, children! God bless you! Today, I've brought this object. What is it called? That's right! It's a wig! Who would like to try it on to see how they look? (You can let one or several children try it on.) Wigs are sometimes used by people who are bald or have little hair. Other times, people use them just for fun or to avoid being recognized. Wigs are often used in plays, soap operas, or movies to portray a character, meaning people dress up to act as someone else. As we've seen today, a wig can make us look different, and if you wear one, it's likely that people who know you might not recognize you.

Application: This wig reminds me of a Bible verse in 2 Corinthians 11:14-15 (read the verse). The passage tells us that Satan can disguise himself as a good angel, just as some people may appear to be good but are actually bad and have no fear of God. Sometimes, even we pretend to be good in front of others, but in secret, we do wrong things. If you've received Jesus into your heart, you should act as a true child of God. If you meet someone who claims to love God but tries to make you do bad things or things that go against the Bible, that person is actually a servant of Satan. Stay away from people like that and don't listen to them.

Invitation: To the non-believing child: Encourage them not to listen to Satan's voice, which seeks harm, but to listen to Jesus, who offers truth and forgiveness. To the believing child: Motivate them to be a genuine believer without pretending.

Memory Verse: 2 Corinthians 11:14

September 21, 2021

THE TRIANGLE

24

Object Lesson 24: The Triangle.

Material: A road safety triangle.

Introduction: Today, I've brought this object that drivers use when their vehicle breaks down on the road. They place it behind the vehicle as a warning sign or even just to indicate that the car is parked. This object is shaped like a triangle. Can anyone tell me, according to math, how many sides does a triangle have? That's right! It has three sides. In mathematics, every geometric shape has a certain number of sides, and in the case of the triangle, it has three. Do you think we can make a triangle with only two sides? (You can use a whiteboard for demonstration.) No, we can't! We need three sides or three lines to form a triangle. If we take away one or two sides, it is no longer a triangle. Similarly, if we add more sides, it also stops being a triangle.

Application: The idea of three sides reminds me of a Bible verse in 1 Thessalonians 5:23 (read it). The apostle Paul prays to God to sanctify his disciples, and it's interesting that he asks God to sanctify three things: spirit, soul, and body. Every person in the world has these three parts, but our eyes can only see one of them. Which one? That's right—the body! The spirit and the soul cannot be seen. The soul is our personality, emotions, and thoughts, while the spirit is what gives life to a person and comes from God. If one of these three parts is missing, a person ceases to exist as such. For example, if we see someone's corpse, it's no longer a person because it has lost the spirit that gives life and the soul. (Read Ecclesiastes 12:7.)

Invitation: Encourage the non-believing child to receive Christ so their soul can be saved from condemnation (the lake of fire). Motivate the believing child to share the message with others and keep their body, soul, and spirit clean.

Memory Verse: 1 Thessalonians 5:23

September 21, 2021

THE TAMBOURINE

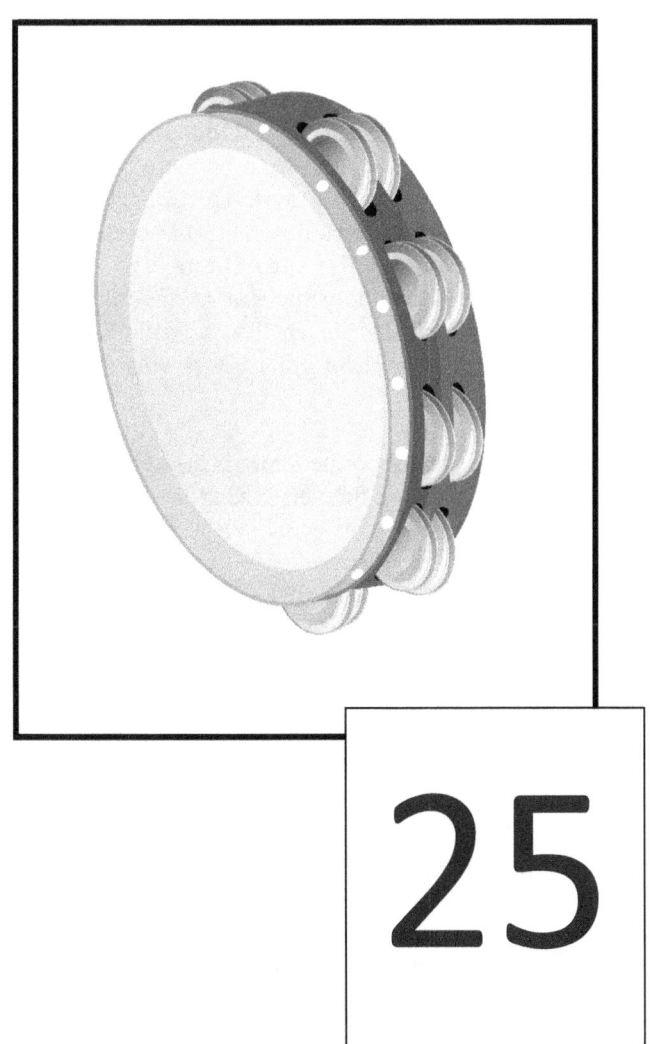

25

Object Lesson 25: The Tambourine.

Material: A tambourine.

Introduction: Hello, children! How are you today? I've brought this object with me. Can anyone tell me what it's called? That's right! It's a tambourine. We can use it to accompany songs of praise to God. Does anyone here know how to play it? (You can allow one or more children to try playing it.) The tambourine is a musical instrument played with the hands, sometimes called a timbrel. It has been around for thousands of years and has often been used in religious activities. The Bible mentions the tambourine multiple times, as it was commonly used in Israel to worship God. People would play it in the temple or other places where they praised the Lord.

Application: This tambourine reminds me of a Bible verse in Psalm 145:2 (read it). In the verse, King David expresses his commitment to praise God every single day. You and I, as children of God, should strive to be like David and worship God daily. How can we do that? (Ask for examples.) We can worship God in different ways, such as singing songs of praise with our mouths, whether at home, on the street, or in church. We can also worship Him through our actions and words because we cannot worship God while also doing or saying bad things.

Invitation: Encourage the Christian child to praise God with both their mouth and heart. Invite the non-believing child to receive Christ so that God can hear their prayers and praises.

Memory Verse: Psalm 145:2

September 21, 2021

THE STETHOSCOPE

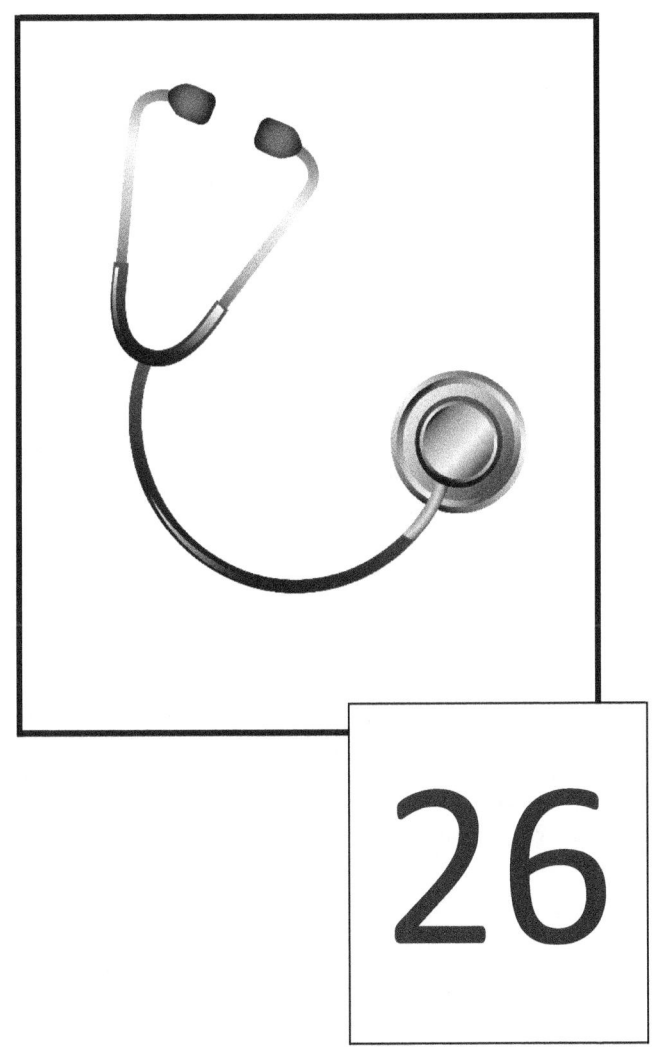

26

Object Lesson 26: The Stethoscope.

Material: A stethoscope (real or toy).

Introduction: Hello, children! Today, I've brought this strange device. Does anyone know what it's called? This is a stethoscope, a tool commonly used in medicine and medical practices. Can anyone tell me who usually uses this device? That's right! Doctors. Doctors have used this tool for many years to listen to the sounds of the heart or lungs of their patients. (You can let the children try using the stethoscope.) As I mentioned, this device is typically used by doctors. And when do people visit doctors? Is it when they're healthy or when they're sick? That's right! Normally, people visit doctors when they are sick.

Application: This idea of doctors and the stethoscope reminds me of a Bible passage in James 5:13-15 (read it). This text encourages us to ask for prayer from the leaders of our church. Just as we think of going to the doctor or taking medicine when we're sick, we should also make it a priority to ask God for healing. If you are a child of God and you feel it's necessary to see a doctor, do so without fear, but always place your trust in God. We can also learn something very important from this passage: not only can God heal our physical illnesses, but He can also forgive our sins, which are like a sickness that leads to eternal death. This eternal death can be avoided by receiving Christ as our Savior.

Invitation: Encourage the non-believing child to receive Christ to be forgiven and cleansed of sin, which is like a sickness that leads to death. Encourage the believing child to pray to God if they are sick or if their heart is filled with sadness and pain.
Memory Verse: James 5:15

September 2021

THE LETTER

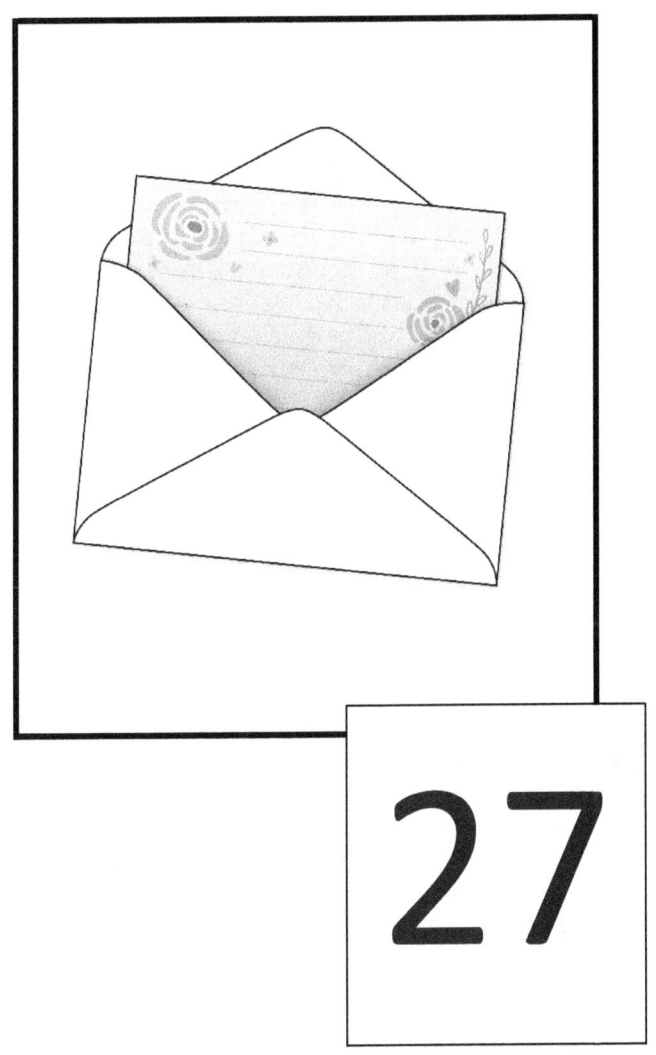

27

Object Lesson 27: The Letter.

Material: An envelope with a handwritten letter inside.

Introduction: God bless you, boys and girls! Today, I've brought this paper envelope with something inside. What is it called? That's right! It's a letter! Since ancient times, people have used letters to communicate with one another. It didn't matter if you were rich or poor, man or woman; anyone who could read and write would write letters or ask others to do it for them. Even young people in love would send letters to express their feelings. Nowadays, people use other means like social media or emails to communicate instead of writing letters. But before these modern tools existed, anyone who wanted to communicate with a family member, a government official, or a business had to write a letter. At first, they were handwritten, then typed on typewriters, and now they're created using computers.

Application: This idea of letters reminds me of a Bible verse in 1 Peter 3:12 (read the verse). It tells us that God listens to the prayers of the righteous—those who love and serve Him. Prayer is the way we communicate with God. You can't send God a letter, call Him on the phone, or email Him, and you certainly can't reach Him through social media. The only way to communicate with God is through prayer. Whether you're alone in your room, speaking out loud, or praying silently in your mind, you can talk to God. You should do this every day because it will strengthen your trust in Him.

Invitation: If you haven't accepted Jesus yet, you can do so today, so that God forgives your sins and listens to your prayers. If you believe in Jesus and have already accepted Him, don't give up—pray every day.

Memory Verse: 1 Peter 3:12

September 2021

THE COUPLE

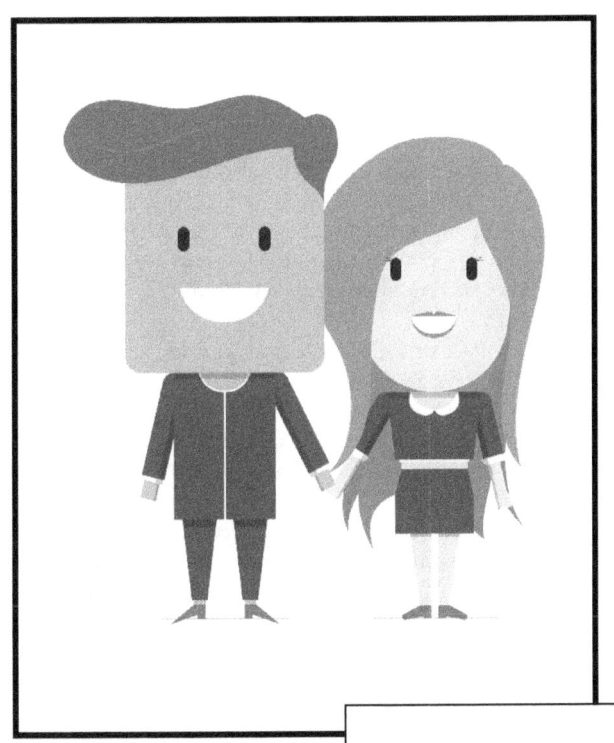

28

Object Lesson 28: The Couple.

Material: A male doll and a female doll (such as a Ken and a Barbie).

Introduction: Hello, kids! How have you been? Today, I've brought these objects. What are they? That's right! A male doll and a female doll, which represent an adult man and an adult woman. One day, all of you will become teenagers, young adults, and then adults. All children like to have different types of toys, and usually, girls have one or more dolls to play with. They also have other toys like toy kitchens, balls, bicycles, and so on, all kinds of toys. Usually, if they have a male doll and a female doll, they play pretend as dad and mom, and sometimes they make a little house to play in. If they have other dolls, they pretend they are the children.

Application: All of this with male dolls and female dolls reminds me of a Bible verse in Genesis 1:27-31 (read the passage). This passage talks about the creation of man and woman. After God created everything that exists, He created man and woman. The Bible says He made them in His image. What does that mean? Is God a man or a woman? "In God's image" means that man and woman are like God, meaning they can feel, think, reason, and tell the difference between good and evil—something that plants and animals cannot do. Man and woman, being made in God's image, are emotionally (in terms of feelings) almost the same, but physically, they are very different. We must also understand that God made man and woman, and He did not create any other type of person. Both of them were commanded to have children and fill the earth.

Application: To the unsaved child: encourage them to receive Christ, recognize that God created them, and that He wants their salvation. To the saved child: encourage them to be sure that one day God will restore the lost paradise, and it will be for the children of God.

Memory Verse: Genesis 1:27

September 2021

THE ARROW

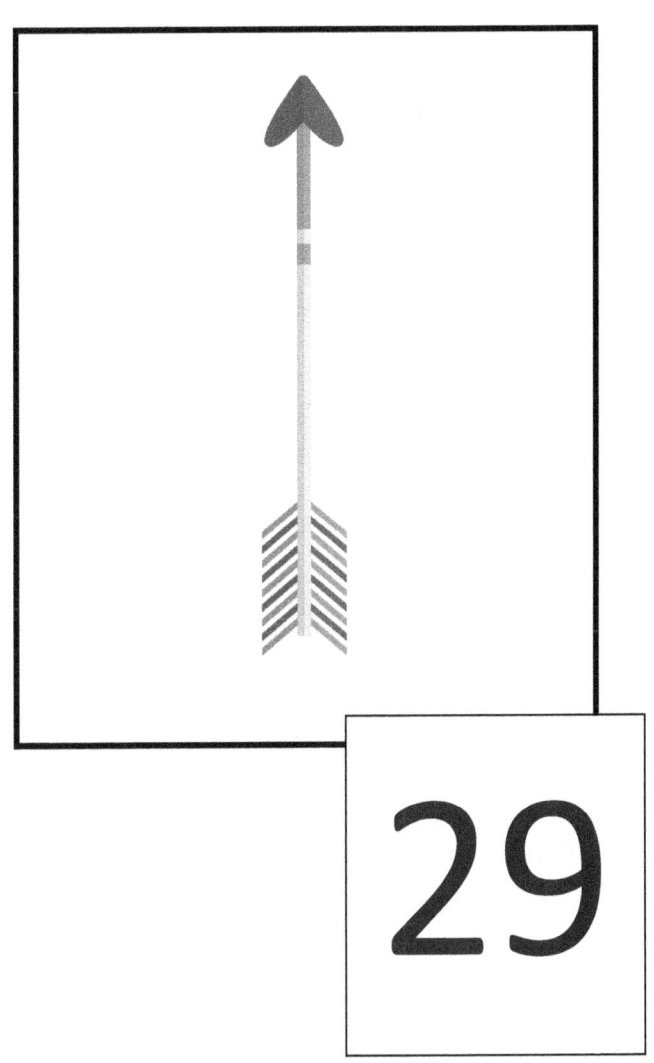

Object Lesson 29: The Arrow.

Material: A toy or real arrow.

Introduction: Hello children! God bless you! Today I have brought this strange object. Does anyone know what it's called? That's right! It's an arrow! An arrow is a projectile shot with a bow, like a very large bullet, and it has been used since ancient times for hunting animals and in warfare. In the beginning, they were made of wood, but now they are made from other materials. Once an arrow is launched, it goes straight ahead until it reaches its target; it doesn't come back, it's not like a boomerang. The arrow continues forward. Good hunters, when using arrows, missed the target very few times. Due to practice and experience, they knew how much force to use and how to hold the bow to hit the target.

Application: The arrow and the hunters remind me of a Bible verse in Hebrews 10:38-39 (read the verse). This verse tells us that those who love God and have received Jesus are the ones who move forward, who do not turn back. What does this mean? It means that if we have accepted Jesus and decided to follow His word, read the Bible, pray, go to church, and more, we will never stop doing it. We should be like an arrow heading toward its target. And what is our target? It's salvation, serving God, and preaching about Christ to others. You and I deviate from the target if we begin to do things that are not pleasing to God (going back means living without Christ, as we did before).

Invitation: To the non-Christian child, encourage them to receive Jesus and follow the target, which is salvation and serving God; to the Christian child, encourage them to stay firm, not to go back to their old life, and to keep moving forward.
Memory Verse: Hebrews 10:39

September 2021

THE ID CARD

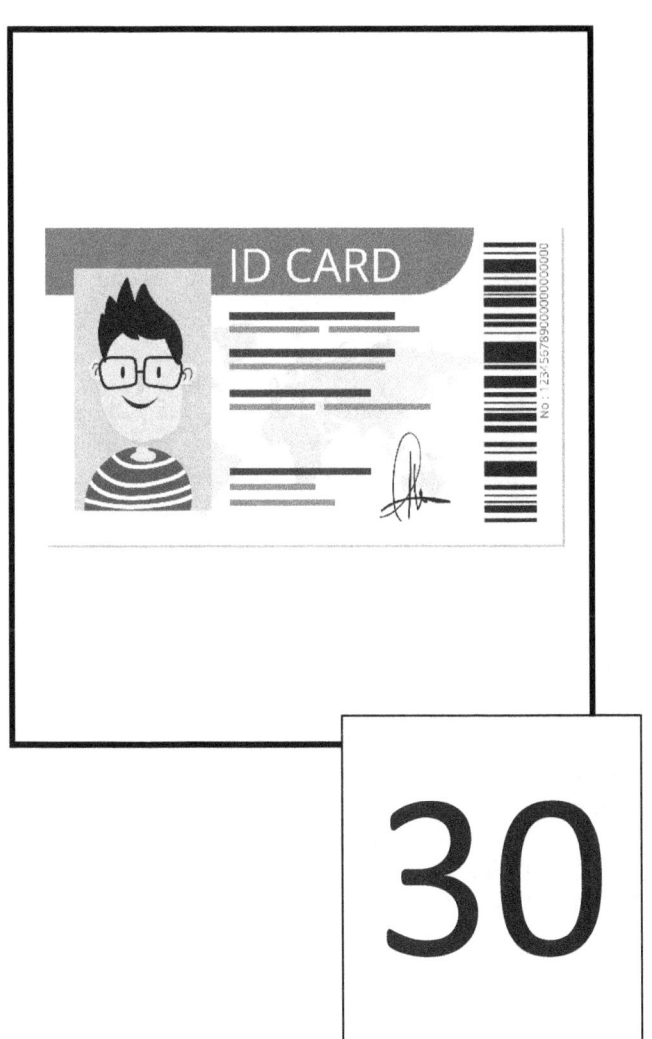

30

Object Lesson 30: The ID Card.

Material: An identification card.
Introduction: Hello children! God bless you! How have you been? Today I've brought this object. Can anyone tell me what it's called? That's right! It's an ID card! Can you tell me what it's used for? (Listen to responses) With the ID card, we can go to a bank to cash checks, make deposits or withdrawals; it also helps us identify ourselves with authorities or apply for a job. We can also use it to vote in government elections. The ID card is a document that proves we are citizens of this country, and therefore, we have certain rights and obligations as citizens of the nation, and it allows us to carry out many transactions.

Application: The ID card reminds me of a Bible verse in Philippians 3:20-21 (read the verse). This verse tells us that all of us who have received Christ and love Him are citizens of heaven. While the ID card identifies us as citizens of this country, spiritually, we are citizens of heaven. Some people seek to obtain citizenship in another country to enjoy certain privileges, but they do not seek the most important citizenship—the heavenly one. If you haven't received Christ, today you can do so, to become a citizen of heaven and be saved from eternal condemnation. We must remember that in this world, we are just passing through, meaning we are here for a limited time.
Invitation: Encourage the Christian child to stay firm in the faith, to understand that we are just passing through and should not cling to the things of this world.
Memory Verse: Philippians 3:20.

September 2021

THE PASSPORT

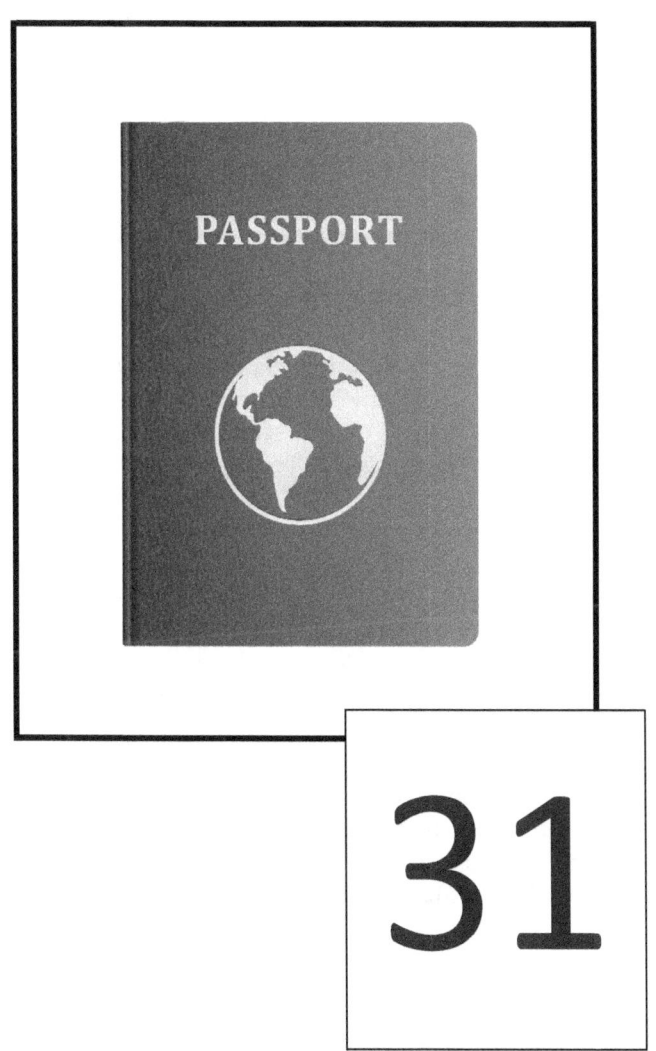

Object Lesson 31: The Passport..

Materials: A passport.

Introduction: Hello, children! God bless you all! Today, I've brought this little booklet; can anyone tell me what it's called? This is a passport, which helps us to leave and enter the country where we live. It's a document we must present when entering another country, along with other documents. If you enter a country without showing it and the authorities catch you, they will send you back to your country of origin. Every country in the world issues passports to citizens who want to travel to another country, but they must meet certain requirements to receive them.

Application: All of this about passports reminds me of a Bible passage in Matthew 7:21-23 (read the passage). In this text, we see that Jesus is clear in saying that not everyone will enter the kingdom of heaven. This means that if we say we believe in God, sing to Him, or do certain things, but we continue to do wrong in His eyes and don't follow His will and word found in the Bible, we won't enter the kingdom of heaven (which will come at the end of the current world when God makes everything new). What is God's will? (Listen to responses.) It's that we believe Jesus is Lord and Savior and accept Him into our hearts, so we can enter the kingdom of heaven (John 3:18).

Invitation: Encourage the unsaved child to receive Jesus, as He is their passport to enter the kingdom of heaven; and encourage the saved child to be grateful to God and share this message with others.

Memory Verse: Matthew 7:21

September 2021

CREDIT CARD

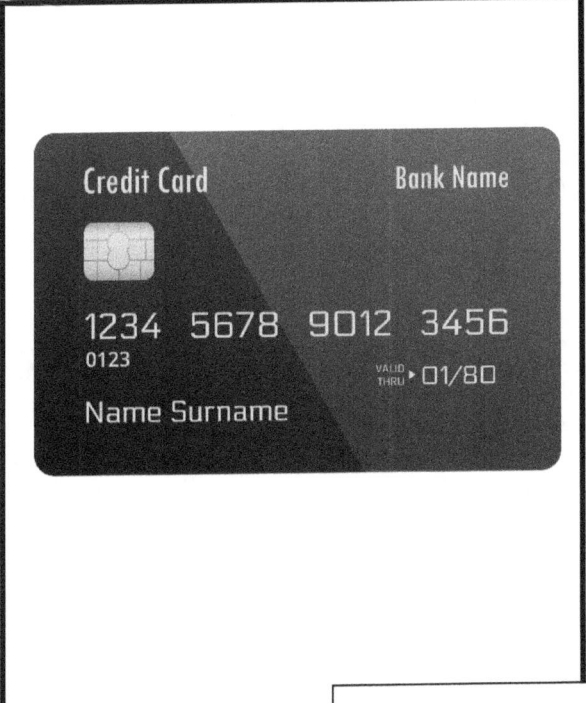

32

Object Lesson 32: Credit Card.

Materials: A credit card.

Introduction: Hello, children! God bless you! Today, I've brought this object—can you tell me what it's called? (Listen to responses.) This object is a credit card. What is it used for? (Listen to responses.) It's used for making purchases at places that accept credit cards. With the card, payments are electronic, so you don't need to carry coins or bills. In ancient times, people used coins made of gold, silver, and other materials. Then paper bills and other materials were created to make purchases or payments. Later, with the rise of science and technology, cards like these were invented to make buying easier. Today, there are many ways to make payments or purchases; it all depends on the place or country where you are. Maybe in the future, there won't be a need for coins, bills, or even credit cards.

Application: This idea of buying and credit cards reminds me of a Bible verse in Revelation 13:14-18 (read the passage). This passage talks about future events that will take place in this world. It tells us that one day, everyone in the world will have to carry a mark on their body, which will be used to buy or sell. Just like today, if you don't have money or a credit card, you can't buy anything, it will be the same in that time. Everyone will be required to have that mark. We don't know exactly what it will look like, but the Bible warns us about it in advance. This will happen when a man sent by Satan rises to rule the world, and he will do so for evil purposes. He will demand that everyone worship him, forget about God, and he will kill those who don't obey him (the Antichrist).

Invitation: If you have not accepted Christ, today you can do so, and God will protect you from anyone who wants to lead you away from Him, deceive you, or cause you to be condemned. Encourage the saved child to stay alert to what's happening in the world and seek God every day.

Memory Verse: Revelation 13:17

September 2021

THE BOAT

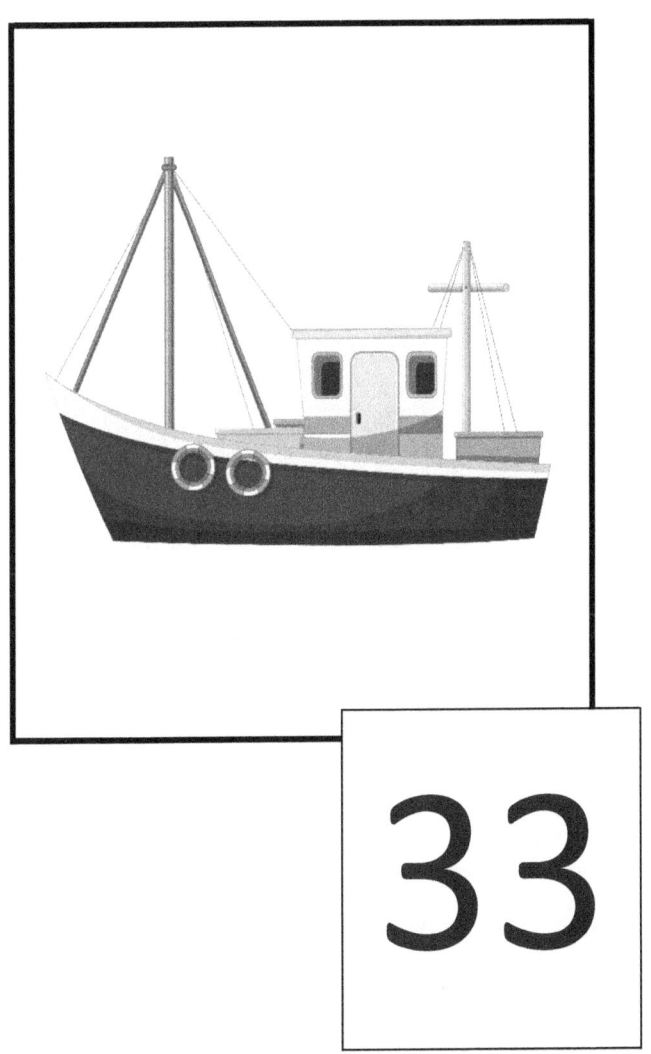

33

Object Lesson 33: The Boat.

Materials: A toy boat.

Introduction: Hello, children! Today, I've brought this object—can you tell me what it's called? That's right! It's a toy boat. How many of you have been on a boat or a small vessel? How many of you would like to ride one? (Listen to responses.) Boats have existed for thousands of years and have been used as a means of transportation to carry objects, people, and animals—basically anything that can be loaded onto it. Where can we see boats? We can see them on large rivers, lakes, and seas. On a boat, we can travel long distances. In ancient times, boats were moved with oars or sails, which were powered by the wind. Later, steam-powered boats were used, and today, boats are powered by engines (steam boats used coal and water, and today, we use oil-based fuels).

Application: Talking about boats reminds me of a Bible verse in Matthew 24:38-39 (read the passage). This passage speaks about ancient times, after God created man and everything that exists. People began to do evil in such a horrible way that God could no longer bear it. So, He decided to send a great flood to the entire world, which would cause the death of all living things: plants, animals, and people. But there was one man who loved God and served Him, and that man was Noah. God had mercy on him and commanded him to build an ark so that he and his family could be saved, along with a certain number of animals.

Application: Encourage the unsaved child to receive Christ, who is like the ark that God sent to save us from future judgment and eternal condemnation because of our sins, just like in the ancient world. Encourage the saved child to persevere and share this message with others.

Memory Verse: Matthew 24:38

September 2021

RUBBING ALCOHOL

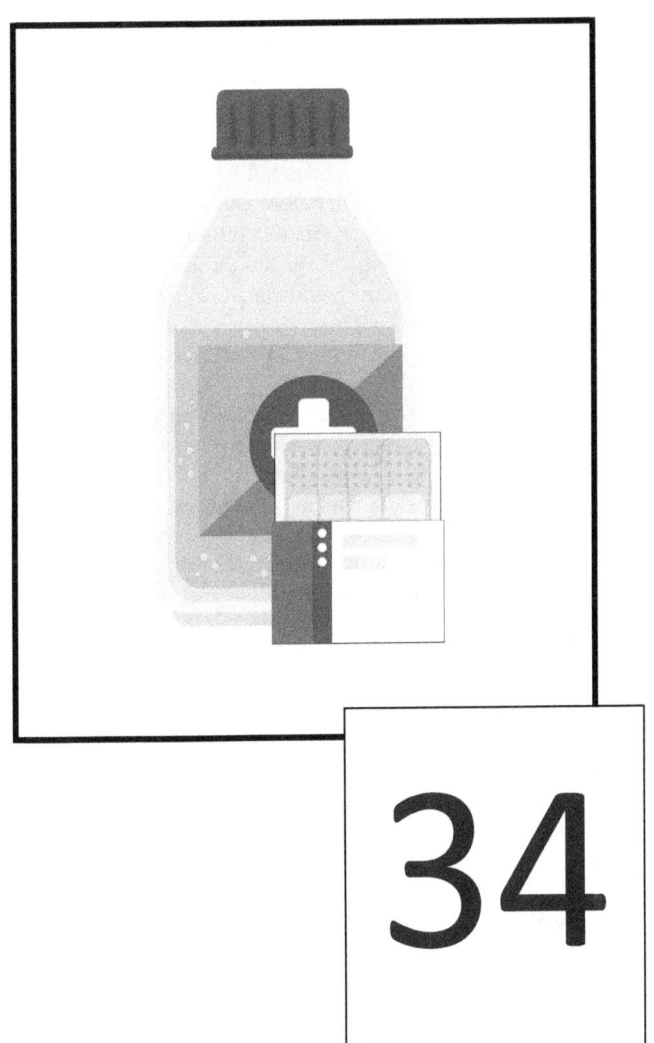

34

Object Lesson 34: Rubbing Alcohol.

Materials: A container with rubbing alcohol (medicinal).

Introduction: Hello, children! God bless you! Today, I've brought this bottle with something inside. Let's open it to smell it and figure out what's inside (you can pass it around to one or more children). This bottle contains rubbing alcohol. Rubbing alcohol is a substance that is commonly used as a disinfectant, meaning it is applied to the hands or other parts of the body to kill bacteria or viruses that can affect our health. For example, before you get an injection, alcohol is first applied to clean the skin. So, this substance, which looks a lot like water, is very important for our health because it helps prevent bacteria from entering our body and making us sick. This is especially important on our hands, because we often touch our mouths with our hands, and that's how viruses and bacteria can enter our bodies.

Application: Rubbing alcohol and bacteria remind me of a Bible verse in 1 John 1:7-9 (read the passage). The text tells us that the blood of Jesus cleanses us from all sin and evil. What does it mean that His blood cleanses us? The blood reminds us of His death on the cross, for He shed His blood when He was whipped and nailed to the cross. All of that was for the forgiveness of the sins of those who believe in Him and receive Him into their hearts. And what is sin? Sin is everything bad we say, think, or do that does not please God. Sin is not something we can remove from our lives with rubbing alcohol or anything else—only by receiving Jesus as our Lord and Savior.

Invitation: Encourage the unsaved child to receive Christ to be cleansed from all sin, and thus be freed from eternal condemnation. Encourage the saved child to ask for forgiveness if they have sinned against God.

Memory Verse: 1 John 1:7-9

September 2021

THE REMOTE CONTROL

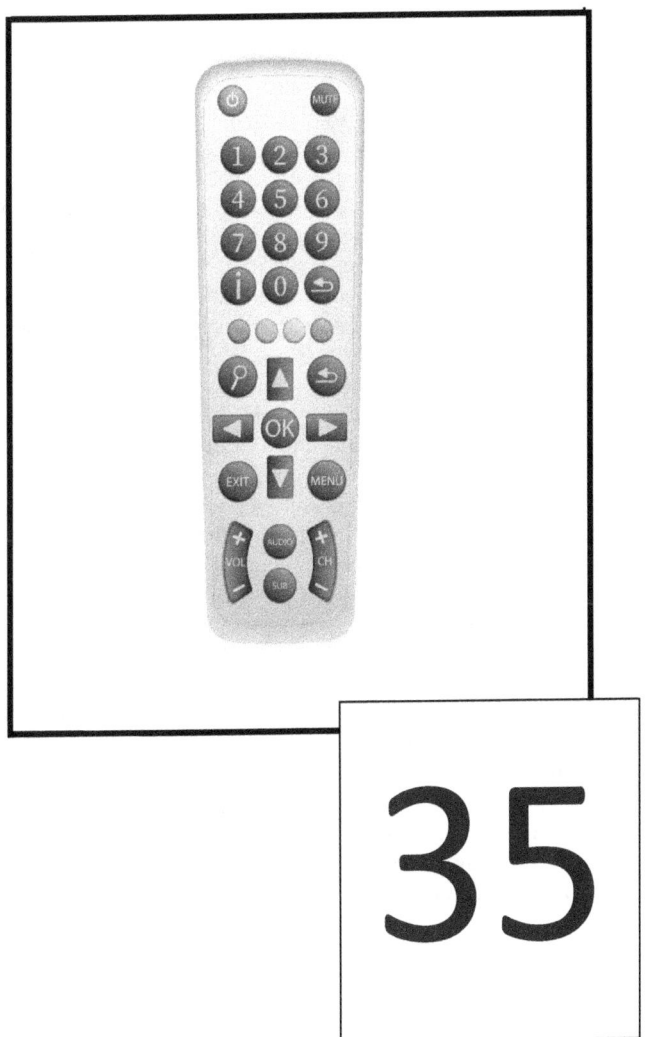

35

Object Lesson 35: The Remote Control.

Materials: A remote control (any kind).

Introduction: Hello, children! Today, I've brought this device—can anyone tell me what it's called? (Listen to responses.) That's right, it's a remote control, and this one is specifically for a television. Nowadays, there are many things that use a remote control, meaning they can be operated from a distance without having to touch them. Can you give me examples of things that use a remote control? (Listen to responses.) There are appliances like: TVs, radios, DVDs, fans, toys, and other things that use remote controls. In the past, many appliances had buttons to turn them on and off, and you had to get up to touch them, either to turn them off or on. But since the invention of the remote control, you don't need to get up or touch anything to turn it off or change the volume. The remote control doesn't need any wires; it works with special rays that we cannot see or touch.

Application: This remote control, which can do things using special rays that we can neither see nor touch, and which can control a device from a distance, reminds me of a Bible verse in Acts 16:16-18 (read it). The text speaks of a young girl who had an evil spirit (a demon) controlling her and making her say things, but God freed her and made the spirit leave her. Spirits are beings we cannot see or touch with our hands, but they can enter someone's body and take control. But if you are a child of God and believe in Jesus, you can be at peace, because they will not possess you. However, they may try to influence or encourage you to do wrong, without even touching you. They can possess an unbeliever and, through them, make you sin, or put things, videos, or people in your path that do not please God (evil spirits are involved in witchcraft, curses, etc.).

Application: Encourage the unsaved child to repent and receive Christ so that God can free them from any evil spirits and protect them from possession and influence. Encourage the saved child to persist in prayer and fasting to resist evil spirits.

Memory Verse: Acts 16:18

September 2021

THE BATTERY-POWERED TOY

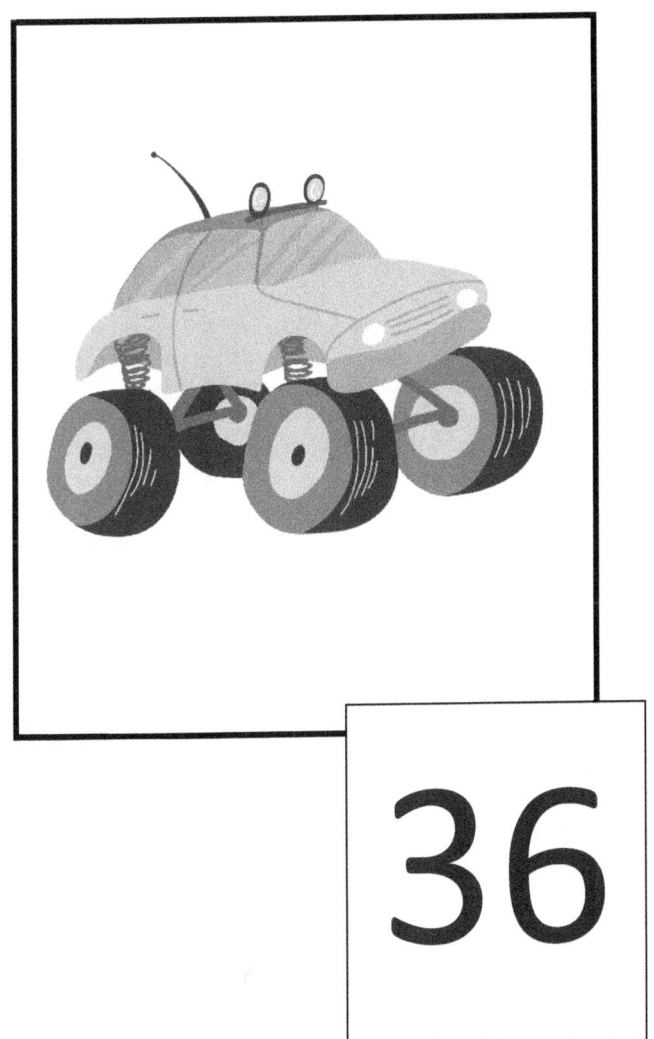

36

Object Lesson 36: The Battery-Powered Toy.

Materials: A battery-powered toy.

Introduction: Hello kids! How are you today? I've brought this object with me. Can you tell me what it's called? That's right! It's a toy car, but this car is not just any toy car. It uses batteries to move and turn on the lights. If I press the power button and there are no batteries, do you think it will turn on the lights or move? If I put paper, plastic, or something else instead of batteries, could it turn on? (Listen to responses, and move to someone who suggests putting paper or something else in the toy instead of batteries.) As we can see, it's really impossible for the toy to turn on the lights or move without the batteries. In fact, it's not just any battery that we need to put in it. This toy uses AAA batteries. They must be this type of battery, and if they are alkaline batteries, even better! It will last a long time.

Application: This idea of batteries and toys reminds me of a Bible verse from Acts 1:7-9 (read it). The passage talks about the moment when the Lord Jesus was saying goodbye to His disciples (since He was going to heaven) and told them that they would receive power once the Holy Spirit came upon them. What was this power about? It was the authority and strength to preach without fear, anywhere and to anyone. They could also pray for the sick, and they would be healed, and even raise the dead. But that power came from the Holy Spirit, not from them. Without the Holy Spirit, they wouldn't have power. They wouldn't have the strength to go preach in Judea, Samaria, and to the ends of the earth. There would be no miracles.

Invitation: I encourage the believer to pray every day and stay in holiness, so that this power will manifest in them. And I invite the non-believing child to receive Christ to receive salvation and the Holy Spirit, and to have the power to do good.

Memory Verse: Acts 1:8.

September 2021

THE DIRTY GLASS

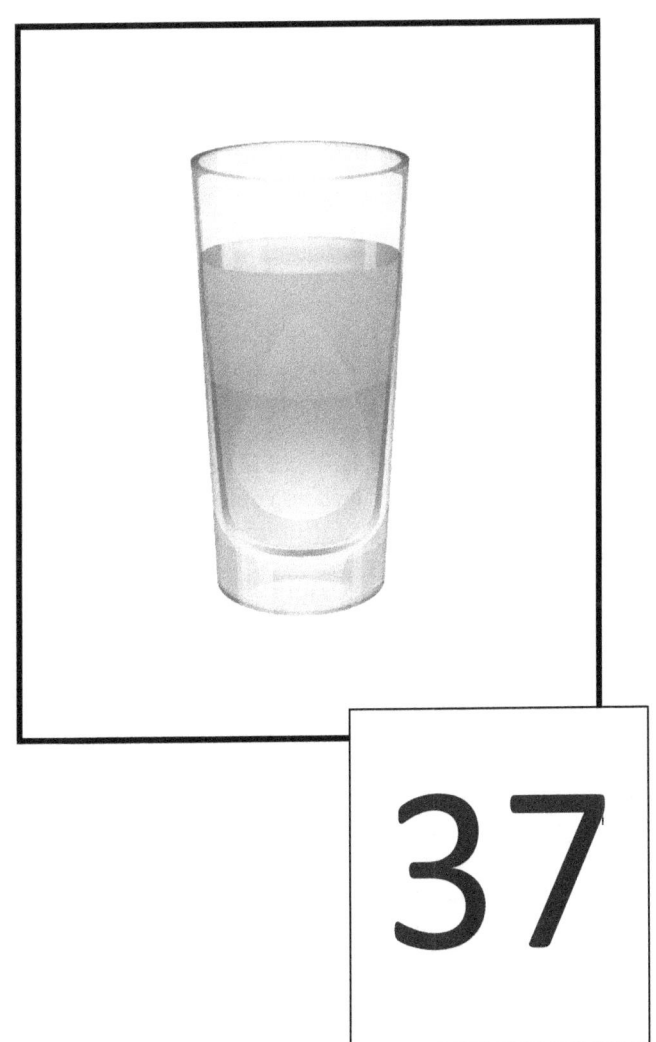

37

Object Lesson 37: The Dirty Glass.

Materials: A clean glass, a dirty glass, and a container of water.

Introduction: Hello kids! God bless you! Today I've brought these two glasses and a pitcher of water, in case anyone is thirsty and wants to drink. (Place the clean and dirty glasses and pass them to one or more children, so they can choose a glass to drink from.) As we can see, no one drank from the dirty glass. Instead, they logically used the clean one, because the dirty glass could have bacteria and substances that might make us sick. That's why every time we use something at home, like a glass or a plate, we always wash it so we can use it again. No one would use a dirty glass or dish.

Application: This dirty and clean glass reminds me of a Bible verse in 2 Timothy 2:19-22 (read the verse). In this passage, there are two interesting points. The first is that God only uses those who cleanse themselves from iniquity. In other words, God can't do anything through you unless you clean your heart every day (ask the children for examples). You won't be able to preach with authority, pray for the sick, and blessings won't come into your life. The second interesting point is that we must associate with those who call on the Lord with a pure heart, which indicates that there may be people who claim to worship God, pray, or even preach, but their hearts are dirty. In other words, they do what's wrong before God, hiding it from others.

Invitation: I encourage the unbeliever to receive Christ so that God can cleanse their heart from sin, granting them forgiveness and eternal life. I encourage the believer to stay clean so that God can use them and they can be worthy of receiving authority and blessings.

Memory Verse: 2 Timothy 2:21.

September 2021

THE CANDLE

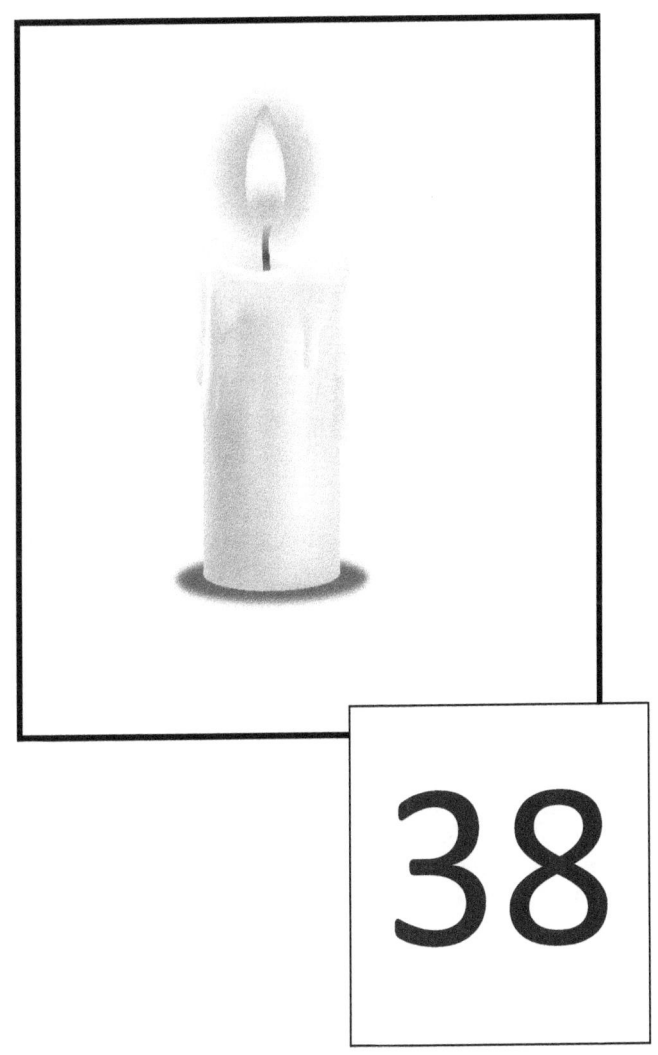

38

Object Lesson 38: The Candle

Materials: Candle and matches.

Introduction: Hello kids! Today I've brought this object with me. Can anyone tell me what it is called? That's right! It's a candle. The candle is used to give us light in the darkness. Maybe in some places, candles aren't used much because they have electricity, and they use light bulbs and lamps to light up at night. But still, candles are used in many places and have existed since ancient times. (Light the candle.) Do you think this small flame could be dangerous? (Listen to answers.) Even though it might seem small, these little flames have sometimes caused big damage, as people who weren't careful left candles burning in places where they shouldn't have, starting fires that burned houses or buildings. Many people have even died from these incidents. And when there are firefighters, they have to go put out the fire.

Application: This candle and the fires remind me of a Bible verse in Revelation 20:12-15 (read the verse). The passage talks about the last times, when everyone will have to give an account to God for all their deeds. The verse is very clear and says that anyone not found in the Book of Life will be cast into the lake of fire. There won't be any firefighters to put out the fire there. Those flames will burn forever, and those who are there will cry forever. They won't be able to die like in the fires we see in this world, because they will be spirits! There is a way to avoid this! What is it? To receive Christ into your heart and repent of your sins.

Invitation: I encourage the believer to be thankful for being in the Book of Life and to talk to others about the danger of the lake of fire. And if someone has not yet believed in Jesus, I encourage them to do so, so that God can forgive them and protect them from that eternal punishment.

Memory Verse: Revelation 20:15.

October 2021

SALT

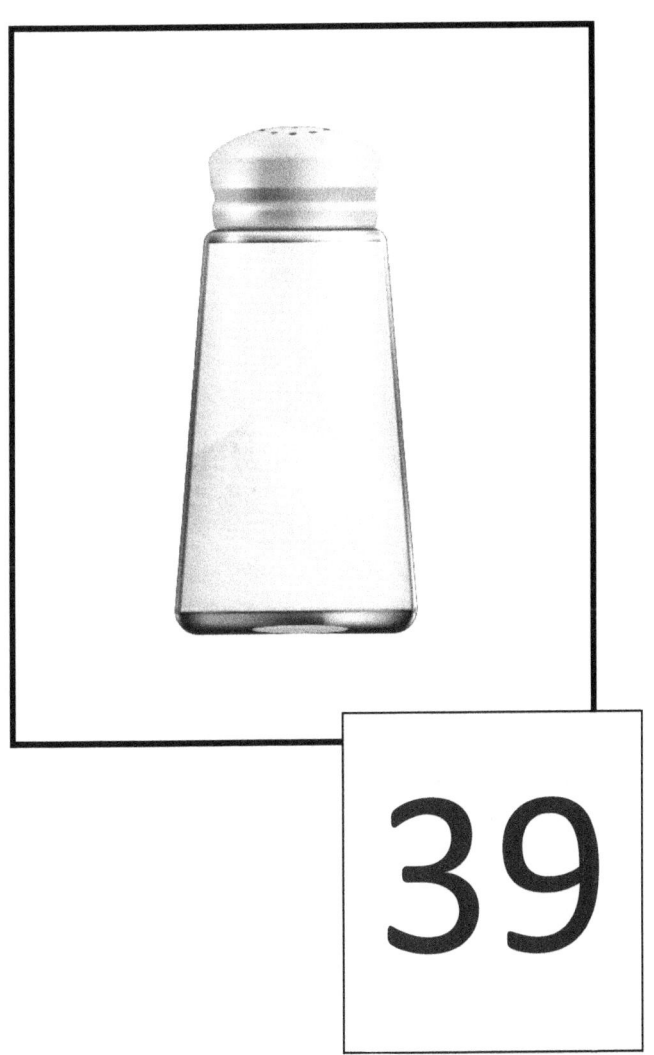

39

Object Lesson 39: Salt.

Material: A small cup with salt.

Introduction: Hello kids! Today I've brought this little cup with something inside. What is it called? That's right! It's salt! Salt is something we all have at home, and it's usually used to prepare food. (You can pass the salt to one or more children to try it.) Sometimes salt is made to look like sugar, but when we taste it, we realize how different they are. Salt usually comes from sea water, but sugar comes from plants. In the past, salt was used to preserve food, like fish, but today we use refrigerators. Salt was highly valued for its ability to preserve food and also for preparing it and enhancing the flavor. For example, we sometimes use salt to eat sour fruits like mango, green jocotes, or oranges. The salt makes them taste better. Would you use salt that tastes like sugar, chili, or something else?

Application: All of this about salt reminds me of a Bible verse in Matthew 5:13 (read the verse). The passage we read are the words of the Lord Jesus, and He speaks metaphorically, saying, "You are the salt of the earth." Who is He referring to when He says, "you"? The Lord is referring to His church, to believers in Christ. What does it mean that we are salt? Just as salt preserves fish from spoiling, we must strive to do good and not let bad things spoil our spiritual lives, or the lives of our family, friends, and country. If we don't oppose what's wrong and we practice it instead, our family and country will suffer, and we will be useless, just like tasteless (flat) salt.

Invitation: I encourage the believer to do good and be the salt of the earth. And I encourage the unbeliever to receive Christ so that sin won't spoil and harm their soul.

Memory Verse: Matthew 5:13.

October 2021

MILK

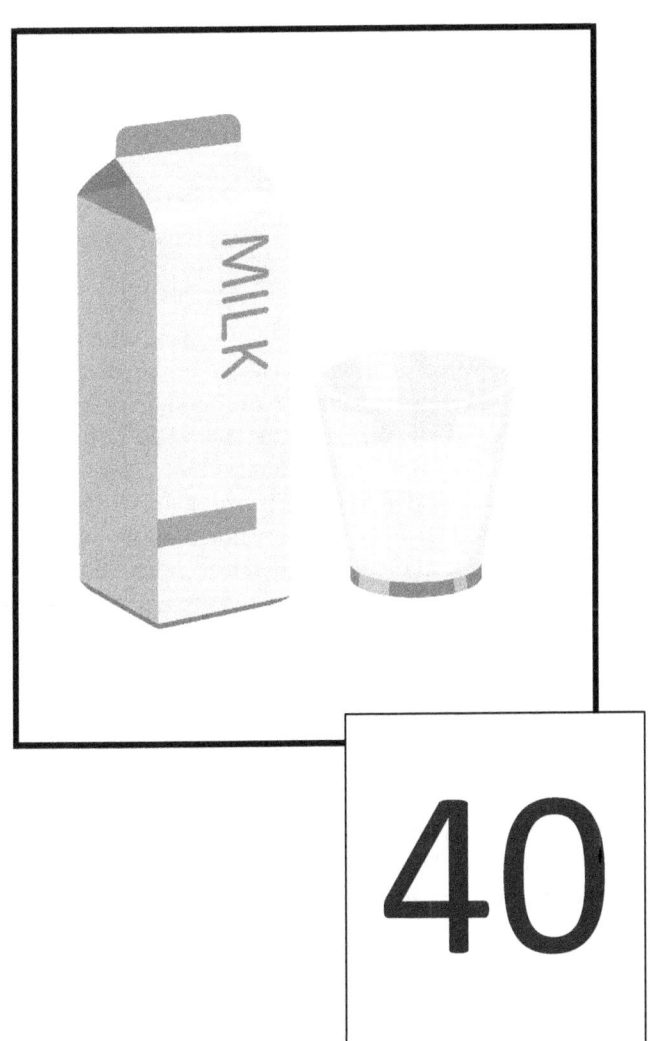

40

Object Lesson 40: Milk.

Materials: A pitcher of milk (and glasses).

Introduction: Hello kids! How have you been? Today I've brought this pitcher with something inside. What is it? It's cow's milk! Who here likes cow's milk? (You can give a little to each child.) Cow's milk is a very well-known drink for us. Milk is used to prepare many sweets and drinks. Can anyone give me some examples? Although we know cow's milk, people also drink milk from other animals like goats, and from plants like soy. Milk is a drink that has existed since ancient times and is still used today.

Application: This milk reminds me of a Bible verse in Exodus 3:7-8 (read the verse). The verse talks about the moment when God spoke to Moses and gave him the good news that He had heard the cries of His people, Israel, who had been enslaved by the Egyptians and had suffered abuse at their hands. Therefore, God decided to free His people from the suffering they were enduring in Egypt. But not only would He free them, He would lead them to a good land, a land flowing with milk and honey. This meant that there were green pastures and an excellent place for raising cattle, which would provide food and produce milk.

Invitation: I encourage the believer to persist, because God will give them a good place to live after the end of times (Revelation 21:1). And I encourage the unbeliever to receive Christ so they can enter the paradise that God has promised to those who love Him.

Memory Verse: Exodus 3:8.

October 2021

THE ROCK

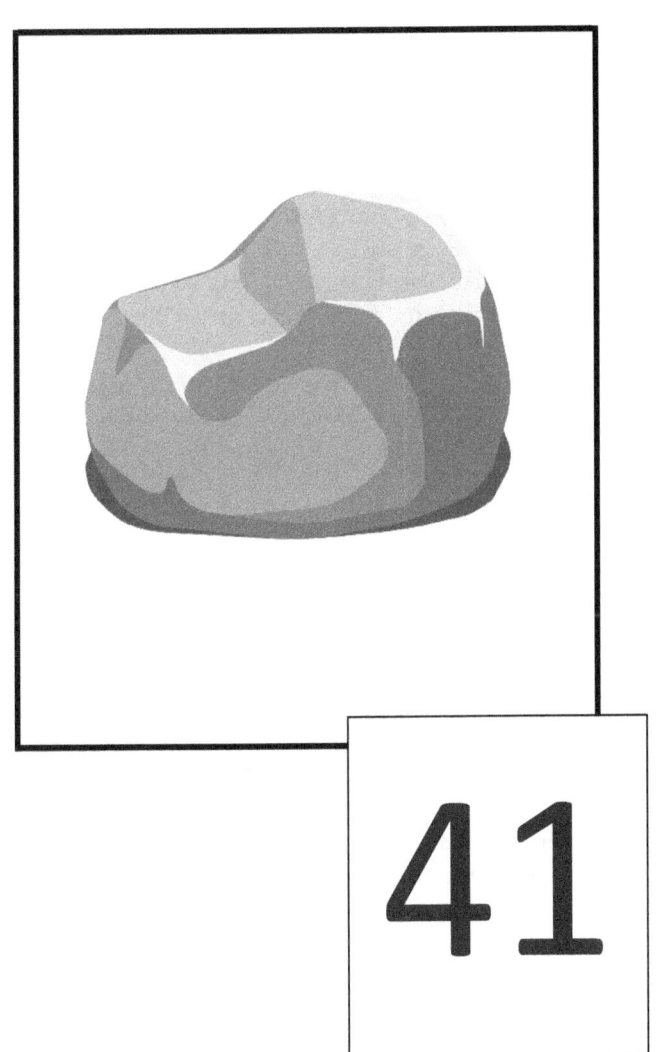

41

Object Lesson 41: The Rock.

Materials: A basket with one or more rocks (stones).

Introduction: Hello kids! Today I've brought this object. What is it called? It's a river stone I found (you can pass it around to the children). Can you tell me what the stone is like? That's right! It's heavy and hard, and if it falls on our toe, it can cause a wound. Stones were used in ancient times to build large structures. Can anyone give me an example? Correct! The pyramids! In places where there are a lot of stones, people build pens for livestock or fences. Do you think that if the pyramids had been made of wood or sand, would they exist today? Of course not! Has anyone made sandcastles at the beach? What happens if the waves reach them? (Listen to responses).

Application: All of this about rocks and sand reminds me of a Bible verse in Matthew 7:24-29 (read the verse). The verse talks about a parable that the Lord Jesus gave (a parable is an example or comparison of one thing with another). The parable talks about two men, one built his house on the rock, and the other on the sand, and then the rains came. Which house fell because of the rain? (Listen to responses). Just like today, great buildings must be built on rock, or the building will sink and fall. What does the parable mean? That everyone who receives Jesus and obeys His commandments will be able to withstand what is bad; otherwise, Satan will come and destroy their life, family, and even the entire country.

Invitation: I encourage the believer to read the Bible and practice its commandments. And I encourage the unbeliever to receive Christ to be protected from evil.

Memory Verse: Matthew 7:24.

October 2021

THE BRANCH

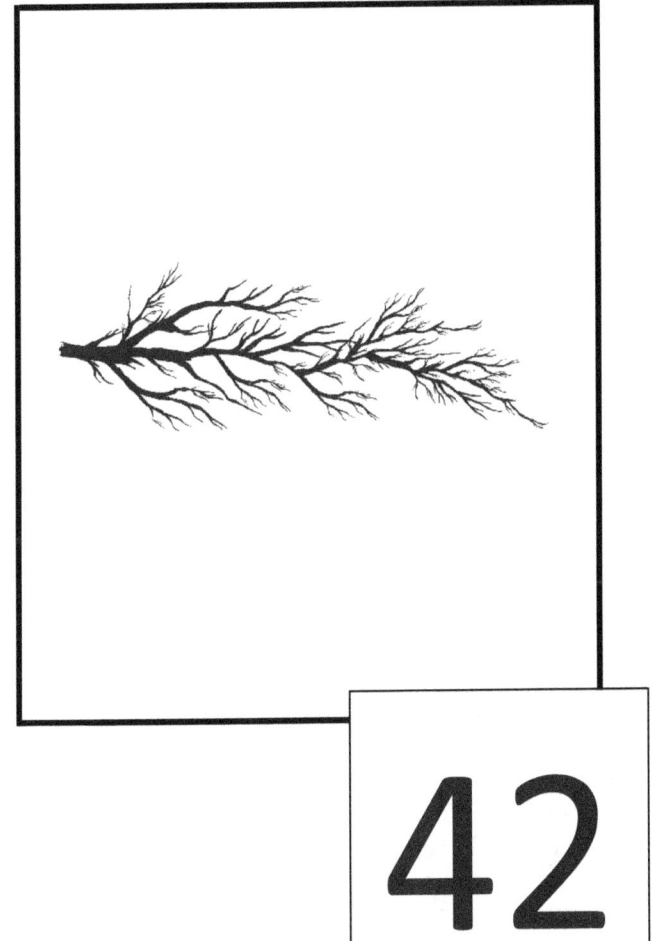

42

Object Lesson 42: The Branch.

Materials: A dry branch.

Introduction: God bless you, children! Today I've brought this object. What is it? It's a dry branch I found. Can you tell me what this branch looks like? That's right! It's dry and without leaves, so it cannot produce flowers or fruit. We all know that branches grow on trees. At first, the branch is a small, delicate shoot that can be easily broken or pulled off. But over time, the branch grows and becomes large, making it difficult to break or cut. To cut it, you would need a machete or a saw. What happens if we cut the branch and throw it aside? That's right! It withers!

Application: This dry branch reminds me of a Bible verse in John 15:4-10 (read the verse). The verse contains words from the Lord Jesus, and He clearly explains that if we cut off the branches of a vine and throw them aside, they wither and are later thrown into the fire. The only way for a branch to grow is by being attached to the tree or plant. The same is true for you and me. We cannot do what is good or be saved apart from God, without believing in Jesus and receiving Him. On the contrary, apart from God, our soul will dry up and be filled with sadness and pain, and in the end, it will be thrown into the lake of fire, just like a dry branch is thrown into the fire. Only with Christ can we grow in what is good and have joy.

Invitation: I encourage the unbeliever to receive Christ in order to grow in what is good and be saved from condemnation. I encourage the believer to remain steadfast in prayer, Bible reading, and fellowship to grow in what is good.
Memory Verse: John 15:5

January 2022

THE DINOSAUR

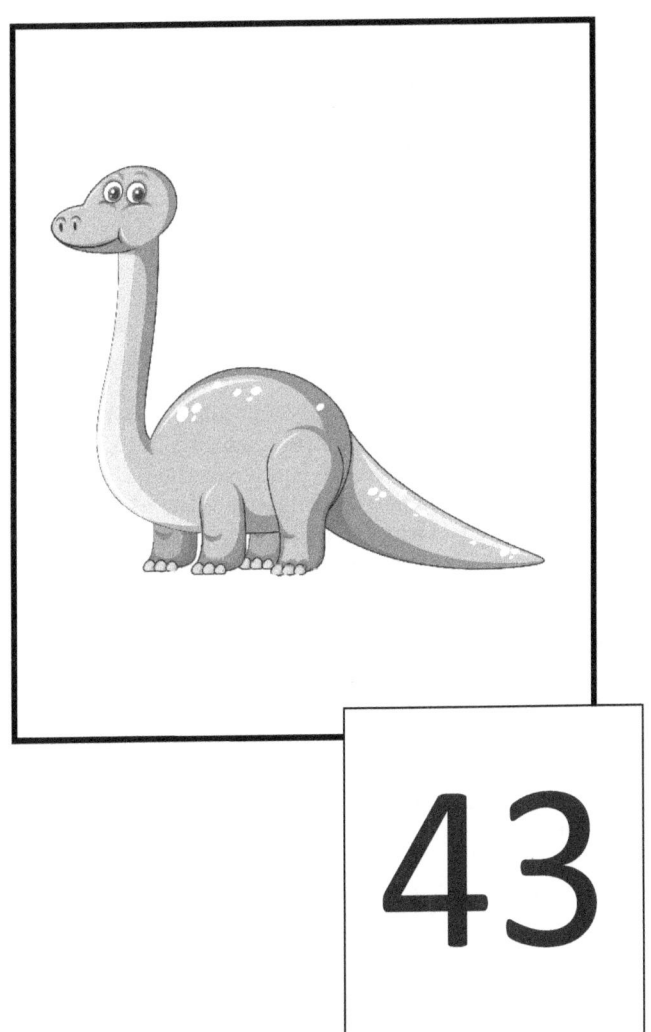

43

Object Lesson 43: The Dinosaur.

Materials: A toy dinosaur.

Introduction: Hello, children! God bless you! Today I've brought this toy. What kind of animal is it? That's right! It's a dinosaur. Dinosaurs are species of animals that no longer exist. Some were giants, but they weren't the only ones. Other types of giant animals have existed that are not dinosaurs, such as mammoths, glyptodonts, paraceratherium, megatherium, and other mammals that are little known but are now extinct. To this day, other types of animals continue to go extinct. Some have gone extinct because people hunt them for food or for their tusks, horns, or skins, as they are valuable. Do you know of any animals that this happens to? (Example: elephants, rhinoceroses, etc.) Other animals have gone extinct because their habitats, such as forests, rivers, or lakes, have been destroyed or contaminated.

Application: All this talk of large and extinct animals reminds me of a Bible verse that describes a large animal, and it's found in Job 40:15-24. The exact animal is uncertain. Some believe it's a hippopotamus, while others think it could be some kind of dinosaur. But yes, we are convinced that great creatures existed and still exist, and we have evidence such as fossilized bones in rocks and other materials. The greatest extinction occurred when God sent the flood because of humanity's sin. Not only animals became extinct, but thousands and thousands of types of plants, insects, and fish were wiped out.

Invitation: To encourage the believer to continue serving God, and to invite the unbeliever to receive Christ to save their soul from a future judgment on those who disobey God, just as it happened during the flood.

Memory Verse: Isaiah 27:1
Other verses: Psalm 91:13, Job 40:1, Job 40:15, Isaiah 27:1

January 2022

POLICE HANDCUFFS

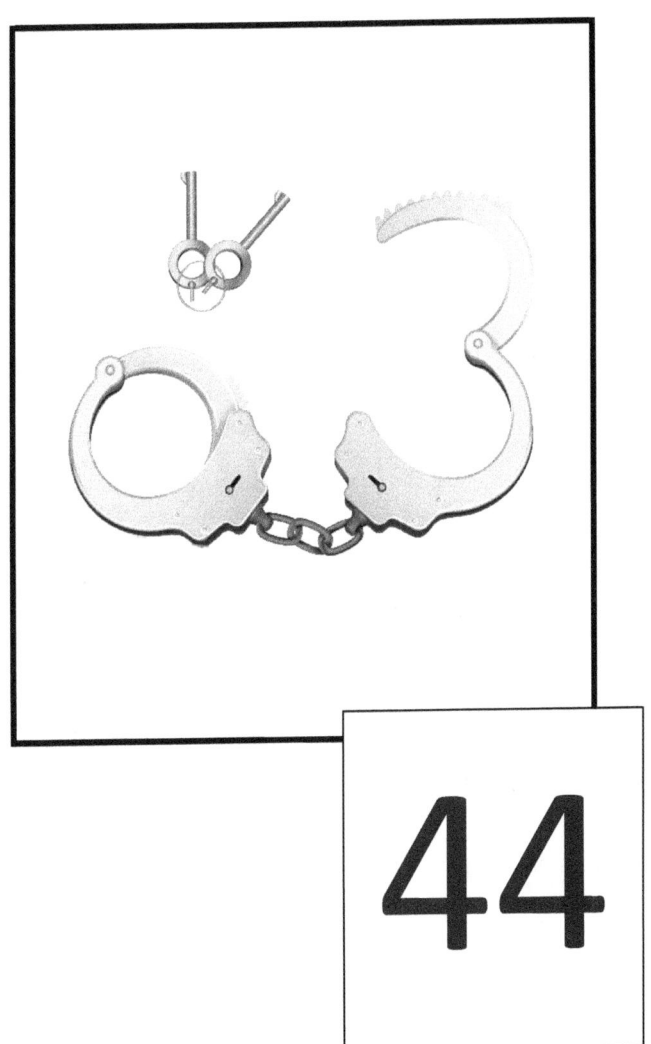

44

Object Lesson 44: Police Handcuffs.

Materials: A pair of toy handcuffs.

Introduction: Hello, children! God bless you! Today, I've brought this object. What is it called? That's right! These are handcuffs! They are an instrument used by the police when they arrest someone. In the past, chains or ropes were used to detain people or prisoners, but today, this object is commonly used to restrain them. Prisoners are people who are accused and sentenced for committing a crime. Crimes are actions that people do that are against the law. In other words, a crime is something that is wrong according to the law, and if someone does it, they must receive a punishment.

Application: All this talk about prisoners and crimes reminds me of a Bible verse in Luke 12:35-40 (read the text). This passage contains words from Jesus, where He warns us about the last times and His coming. But He also makes us reflect that we should always be ready to do good, whether He comes tomorrow or in a thousand years. Our bodies are not eternal, and one day we will die. Death can surprise us like a thief coming at night when we least expect it. If we die without repenting and receiving Christ, there will be no second chance. Some people live doing evil things, trusting that Jesus isn't coming, but everything has consequences. Just like a thief, He will come when we least expect it.

Invitation: Encourage the unbeliever to receive Christ as soon as possible because we do not know what the future holds. Encourage the believer to avoid doing wrong and to always be attentive to doing good.

Memory Verse: Luke 12:40

October 2021

THE FACE MASK

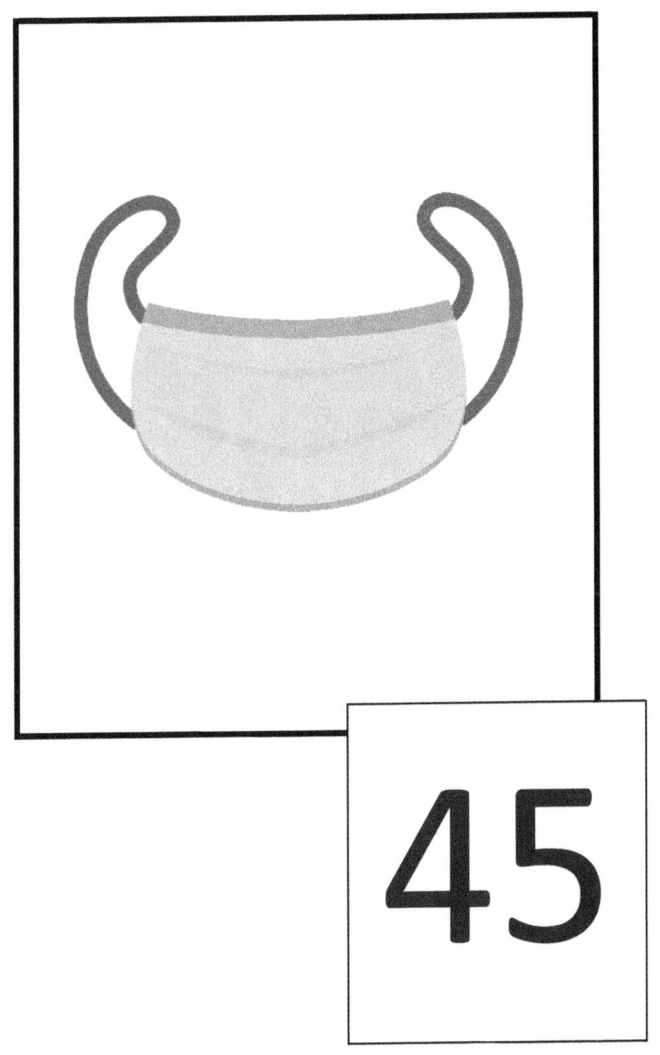

45

Object Lesson 45: The Face Mask.

Materials: A face mask.

Introduction: God bless you, children! Today, I've brought this object. Can you tell me what it's called? That's right! It's a face mask! Can you tell me what it's used for? The face mask is used to protect our respiratory system from dust or viruses that can enter through the nose and mouth, and then to the lungs. Face masks are usually worn in hospitals or construction sites, where there is dust or fine particles (in hospitals, face masks and gloves are used to protect against germs). People also wear them to avoid spreading saliva to others, as when we speak, we expel saliva, and if we're sick, we can pass the virus or bacteria to someone else.

Application: All this talk about face masks and viruses that can make us sick and even lead to death reminds me of a Bible verse in Acts 13:36-39 (read the text). The verse tells us that the forgiveness of our sins is only through Jesus. Sin is the bad things we say, think, or do. Do you think that if we wear a face mask, it can help us avoid sin? Of course not! The Israelites, or God's people, tried (before Jesus came) to be saved by following the law of Moses, but they couldn't fulfill it completely. Likewise, sometimes we do things thinking they will make us saved, but no, it's only possible by receiving Jesus and repenting of our sins.

Invitation: To the unbelievers, encourage them to receive Christ to receive forgiveness, and to the believers, motivate them to remain firm, spreading the message of Christ to others.

Memory Verse: Acts 13:38-39

October 2021

THE TEDDY BEAR

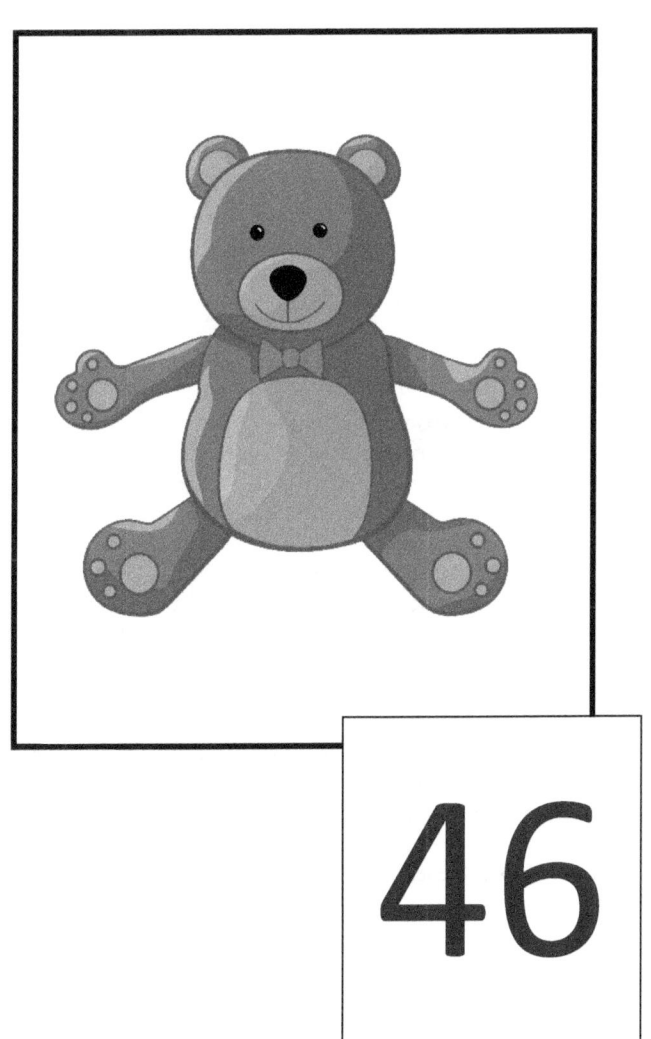

46

Object Lesson 46: The Teddy Bear.

Material: A teddy bear (or another animal).

Introduction: Hello, children! How have you been? I'm glad to see you! Today I've brought this object. Can anyone tell me what it is? Correct! It's a teddy bear. Who likes teddy bears? This little bear looks very cute and friendly, but real bears that live in the forest are very dangerous. If you're in their territory, they can hurt or even kill you. Bears walk on four legs, move on the ground, and can climb trees, so if you try to escape, it's useless. In fact, some bears even go into rivers or lakes to search for food. Do you know what bears eat? (Listen to responses) While some bears can swim a little, they can't do it for long because they aren't adapted to swim all day.

Application: All this talk about bears and water reminds me of a Bible verse in Genesis 7:16-10 (read the text). This passage is very well known by everyone. It talks about the great flood that came upon the Earth, but God saved Noah, his family, and a pair of certain animals that couldn't swim. The fish, however, didn't enter the ark because they could swim. Among the animals that entered the ark was a pair of bears, which is why bears exist to this day. The other people and bears that didn't enter the ark perished. That flood was a punishment that came because of the wickedness of humanity. People were so evil that God could no longer tolerate such wickedness. Today, the world is the same, but God has other judgments prepared for this world.

Invitation: To the unsaved, encourage them to receive Christ, just as Noah entered the ark to be saved. To the saved, encourage them to preach to their friends and family to protect them from judgment.

Memory Verse: Genesis 7:10.

January 2022

THE TOOTHBRUSH

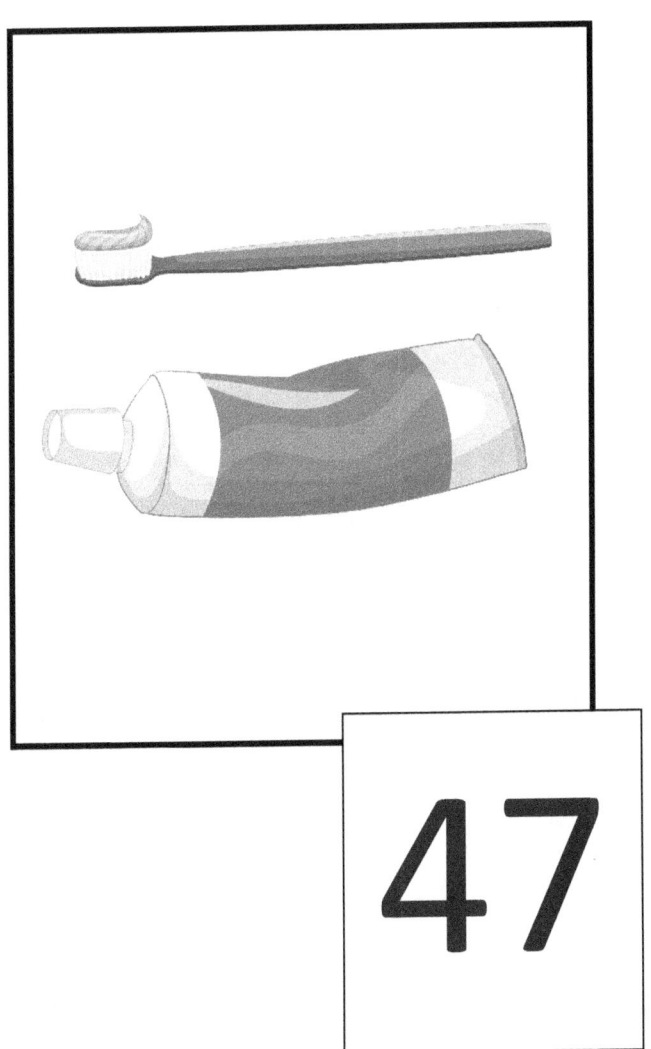

47

Object Lesson 47: The Toothbrush.

Material: A toothbrush and toothpaste.

Introduction: God bless you, children! Today I've brought these objects. What are they called? That's right! It's a toothbrush with toothpaste. Who has a toothbrush? How many times a day do you brush your teeth? (Listen to responses) The toothbrush has been used for many years to clean food particles from our teeth. If we don't do this, our teeth will get cavities, and cavities damage the teeth and can cause pain, even leading to tooth loss. Along with the toothbrush, we use toothpaste, which contains substances that help keep teeth clean and shiny. Toothpaste is not something new, as some ancient civilizations invented products similar to toothpaste.

Application: All this talk about clean teeth and toothbrushes reminds me of a Bible verse in Matthew 5:8, Proverbs 22:11, 20:9 (read the texts). These verses talk about the cleanliness of the heart. In this case, the heart doesn't refer exactly to the organ that pumps blood, because we can't dirty it with our hands or clean it with a toothbrush or rag—this heart is always clean. The heart the Bible speaks of is our soul, what we feel, which we cannot see or touch. How can we clean our soul? (Listen to responses) We can do this by receiving Christ, then reading the Bible, praying, and going to church. Only Christ can cleanse the heart, no one else.

Invitation: To the unsaved child, encourage them to receive Christ to be cleansed and receive forgiveness for their sins and salvation. To the Christian, encourage them to keep their heart clean by avoiding doing, saying, or thinking bad things.

Memory Verse: Proverbs 20:9.

January 2022

THE BOX AND THE LIGHT

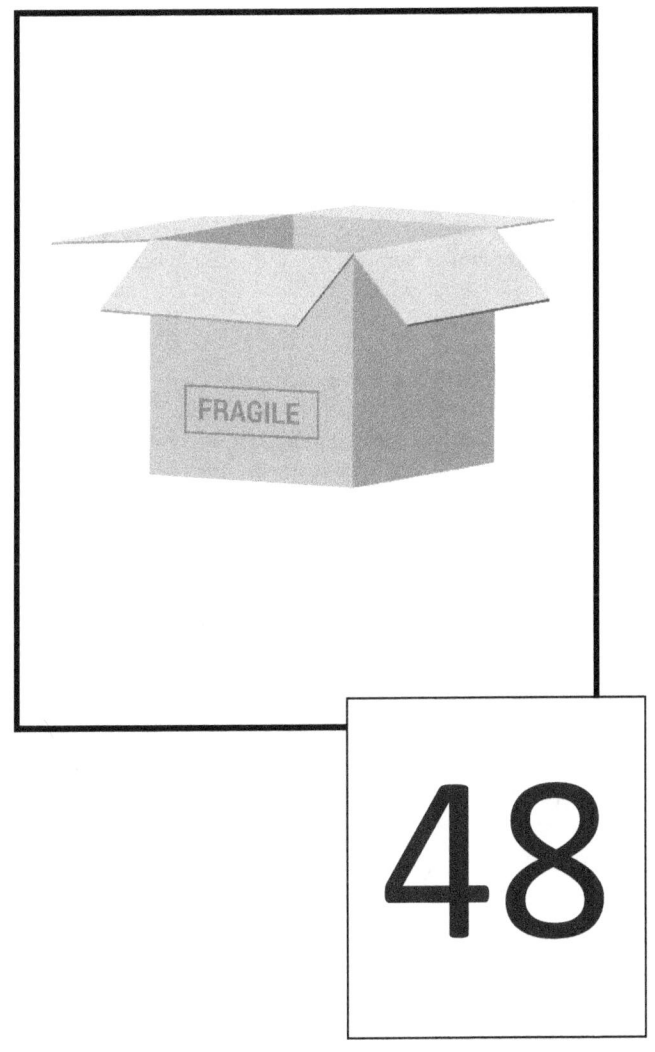

48

Object Lesson 48: The Box and the Light.

Material: A box and a candle (or a small light).

Introduction: Hello, children! God bless you! How are you? Today I've brought these objects. What are they? That's right! It's a candle and a box! We all know candles, and we've used them at some point. They are used for different activities, come in various colors and shapes, and are usually used for religious purposes or to light up a place. Before electricity existed, candles were essential for lighting homes or any building. Today we have light bulbs and lamps, which are installed on ceilings or walls, but candles are never placed on the floor, let alone under something. (Light the candle) Let's put the candle under the box. What happened? What do you think? (Listen to responses).

Application: This talk about candles and lights reminds me of a verse in Matthew 5:14-16 (read the text). The text tells us that if someone lights a candle, they don't put it under a box, especially at night! It is placed up high. What does that mean? It means that if you and I have received Christ, we should be a light in this world. How? By following God's law and preaching Christ. Therefore, we cannot hide and deny our faith. If we don't speak of Christ and do what is wrong, we will be like a candle under a box, and that doesn't please God. If you have received Christ, you should not hide it from your friends and family; they need to know. The first place your light should shine is with your family and friends.

Invitation: To the unsaved child, encourage them to receive Christ so they can be a light and be saved from eternal darkness. To the Christian child, encourage them to be a light without fear, as God will reward them.

Memory Verse: Matthew 5:16.

January 2022

THE ROD

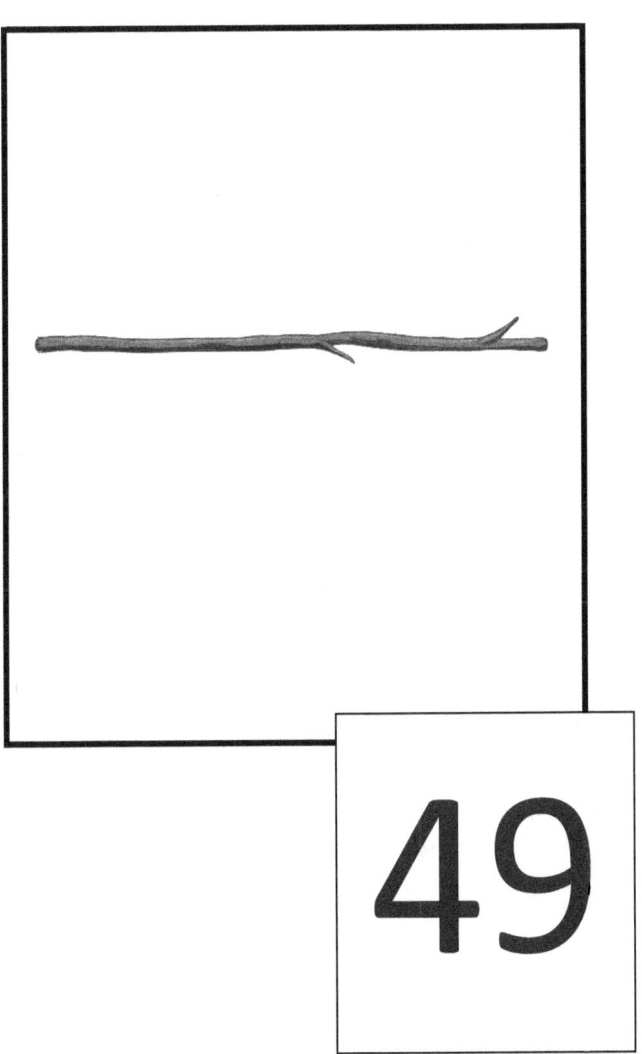

Object Lesson 49: The Rod.

Material: A rod (a long rod, typically made from a branch) (a belt can also be used).

Introduction: Hello, children! How are you? I've brought this object. What is it? It's a rod! That's what my grandparents used to call it (it's a thin branch less than a centimeter in diameter). It is made from branches, and the rod was used for many things, including disciplining the children in the house, meaning their own children. Some people use other objects to discipline their children, such as belts. Discipline is applied when children deliberately and intentionally defy the authority of their mom or dad. No one likes being disciplined, but God placed people in charge of correcting us so that we don't do whatever we want. At home, that's our parents, and at school, it's the teachers. When we grow up, the authorities of the country, like judges and police officers, are in charge of us.

Application: All this talk about the rod and discipline reminds me of a Bible verse in Proverbs 29:15-17 (read the text). The text we've read is clear: when our parents correct us properly, we will be good citizens and not bring shame to our parents. On the other hand, if they don't correct and discipline us, we will become disrespectful and irresponsible. There are times when our parents need to set punishments and limits for our disobedience, and even discipline us with a rod if we intentionally choose to challenge them. If they didn't do this, we would later do the same to our teachers, the police, and our bosses. Then, God will punish us for our wrongdoings, and we will be worthy of eternal condemnation.

Invitation: To Christian children, encourage them to respect their parents and obey God, as it is written in the Bible. To the unsaved child, encourage them to receive Christ to receive salvation and avoid eternal punishment in the lake of fire.

Memory Verse: Proverbs 29:15.

January 2022

THE STAINED SHIRT

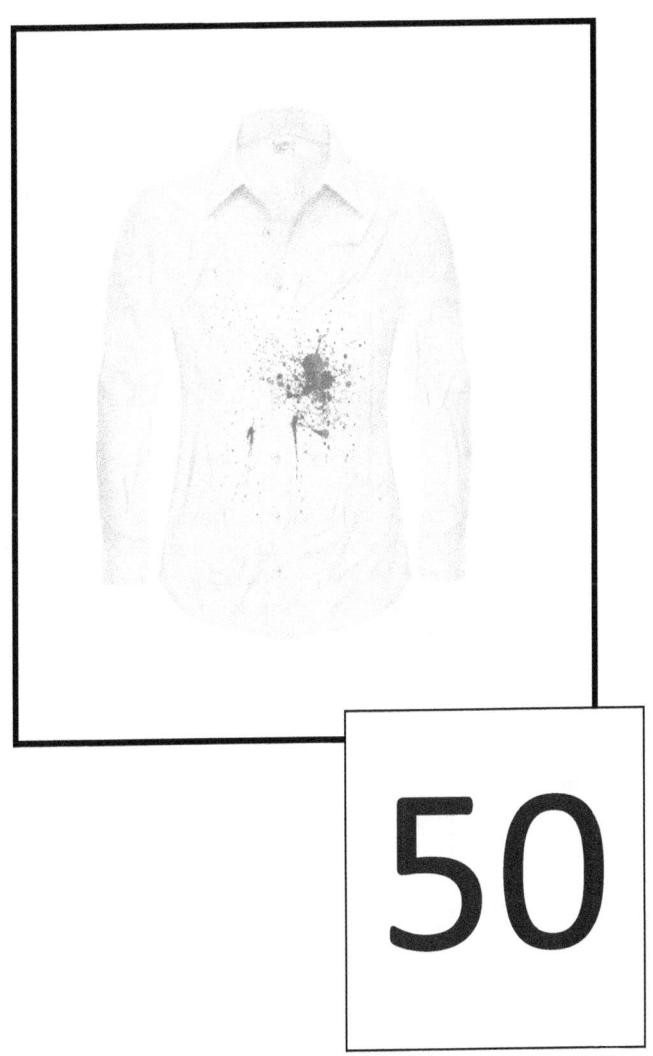

Object Lesson 50: The Stained Shirt.

Material: A stained shirt.

Introduction: Hello, children! God bless you! Today, I've brought this object. What is it? That's right! It's a shirt! The shirt is very nice, and I used to wear it to many places, especially to church to praise God. I also wore it to other important activities. I'm going to put on the shirt so you can see how it fits me (put the shirt over the t-shirt). Do you think it fits me well? How does it look? (The children should be able to identify one or more stains on the shirt). Do you think I can wear this shirt to church or to an important meeting? Of course not! If we're going to go to an important place or activity, we need to dress appropriately. We can't go with stained, dirty, or wrinkled clothes.

Application: All of this about the stained shirt reminds me of a Bible verse in Revelation 3:4-6 (read the text). The text talks about a promise from the Lord Jesus, where He says He will give white garments to those who overcome, that is, to everyone who has received Christ and continues every day of their life in prayer, Bible reading, attending church, and keeping God's commandments. The Bible also makes other references where it tells us that we shouldn't have spots or wrinkles on our garments. Is it talking about our clothes? No! It's talking about our hearts, our souls, our lives. How can the heart be stained? Through sin. These are stains, meaning the wrong things we think, say, or do that don't please God (read Ephesians 5:27).

Invitation: To the unsaved, encourage them to receive Christ to be cleansed from all sin, and to the saved, encourage them to remain clean and not practice sin.

Memory Verse: Revelation 3:5.

January 2022

THE JEWELS

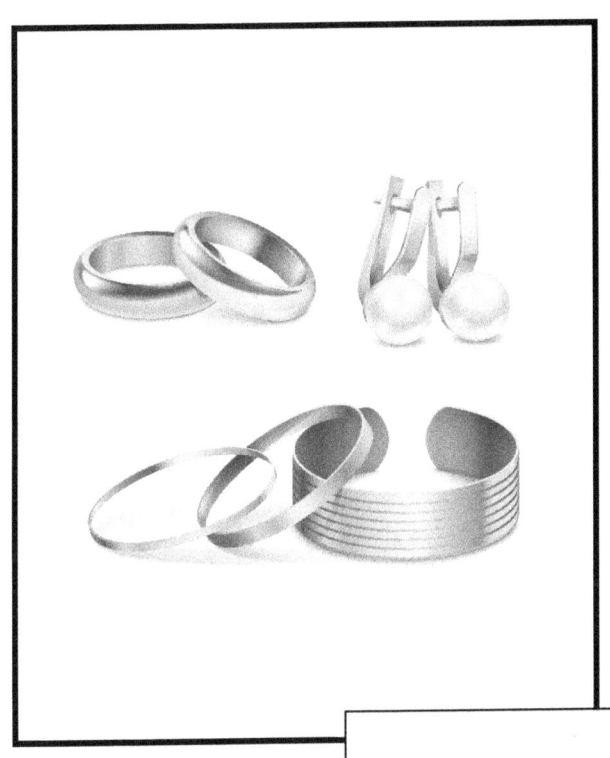

51

Object Lesson 51: The Jewels.

Material: Rings, earrings, and/or bracelets.
Introduction: Hello, children! How are you? Today I've brought these very beautiful objects. What are they called? These jewels were lent to me by my wife. They are very valuable and are used for special occasions. Does any girl want to come up and try them on? (Pass them to one or more girls.) How do the jewels look on her? They look great! Jewels make women look more presentable and enhance their beauty. It's also important to note that jewels are of great value, usually made of gold and silver. Sometimes, other very expensive materials like diamonds and pearls are added. Now, let's cover these jewels in mud. Does anyone want to wear them now? (The children should respond that they do not.)

Application: All of this talk about jewels reminds me of a Bible verse in Proverbs 11:22 (read the text). The verse tells us that a woman or girl (this also applies to boys) who considers herself beautiful but walks away from reason (who does wrong things, doesn't think properly about what they do, and lives apart from God) is like a gold ring in the snout of a pig. Would you give these jewels to a pig to wear and get them all dirty? Of course not! We don't give our jewels to animals because they don't understand their value or how to take care of them. You and I are like jewels in God's eyes, but if we do wrong, we are like jewels in the snout of a pig.

Invitation: To the Christian child, encourage them to stay firm, not to do wrong, and to the unsaved, encourage them to receive Christ so they are not in the hands and snout of Satan.
Memory Verse: Proverbs 11:22.

January 2022

THE FLOWERS

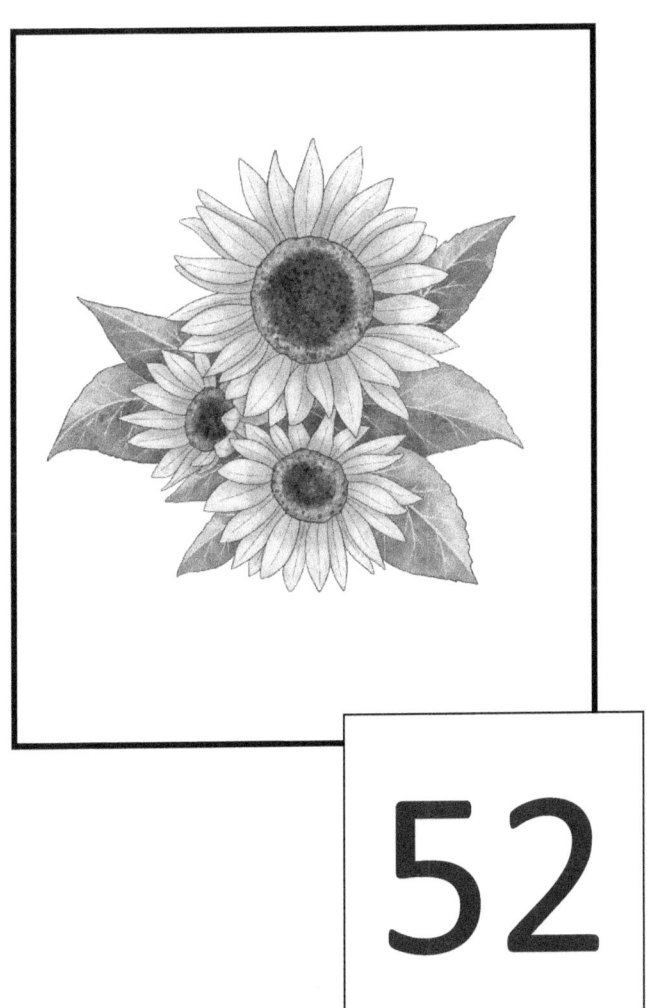

52

Object Lesson 52: The Flowers.

Material: Flowers (natural or artificial).
Introduction: Hello, children! God bless you all! Today I've brought these objects. What are they called? That's right! They are flowers! I picked these beautiful flowers from my garden. These flowers are from a plant called sunflower (mention the type of flower you've brought). Almost all plants produce flowers, and flowers come in various sizes, colors, and shapes. Some have very fragrant scents, like roses and lemon balm. Some flowers produced by plants are purely ornamental, while others are an indication that the plant will produce fruit. All around the world, people buy flowers to give as gifts or to decorate their homes. In some countries, like ours, flowers are also used at funerals. In short, flowers are everywhere, especially in gardens and forests.

Application: All of this talk about flowers, plants, and trees reminds me of some Bible verses in Revelation 2:7, 21:1-4 (read the texts). These verses talk about something in the future. They speak of the tree of life and a paradise that God has prepared for all those who love Him. What is so special about that paradise? According to the Bible, in that paradise, we will be able to eat from the fruit of the tree of life, though no one knows exactly what it looks like. You and I will see it if we have received Christ and obey Him. But in that paradise, we won't only be able to eat that fruit; God has promised that there will be no more weeping, crying, pain, or death, things we have to endure today. It is important to note that anyone who does wrong and does not love God will not be able to enter that paradise.
Invitation: Encourage the unsaved child to receive Christ to enjoy that paradise, and encourage the saved child to stay firm and thank God for that paradise and the eternal life He has given us.
Memory Verse: Revelation 2:7.

January 2022

ABOUT THE AUTHOR

Brother José Jáenz was born on January 22, 1984, in Managua, Nicaragua. He accepted Jesus as his Lord and Savior at the age of 15. After being baptized at the age of 16, he began his service in the work of God, in children's clubs or cells. He also volunteered in two internationally known Christian ministries, APEN (Alliance for the Evangelization of Children) and Compassion International, both very important for his spiritual growth, where he received multiple trainings and courses in Bible teaching for children, among other topics. He also studied at the Etheridge Evans Nicaraguan Bible Institute in Managua. Since the beginning of his faith journey until today, he has also worked in other areas of God's work, though to a lesser extent, such as the diaconate, men's ministry, Sunday school teacher, among others. He is currently married with two daughters and spends part of his time writing and preparing materials for Bible teachers.

GET YOUR PHYSICAL OR DIGITAL COPY

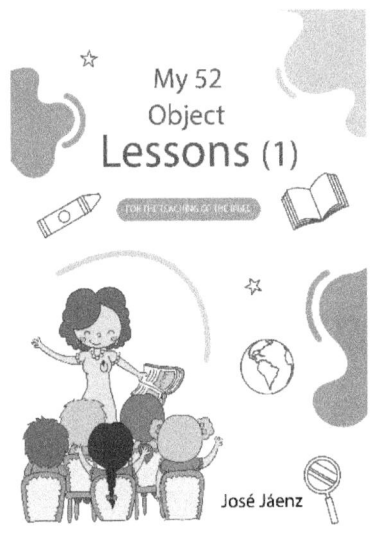

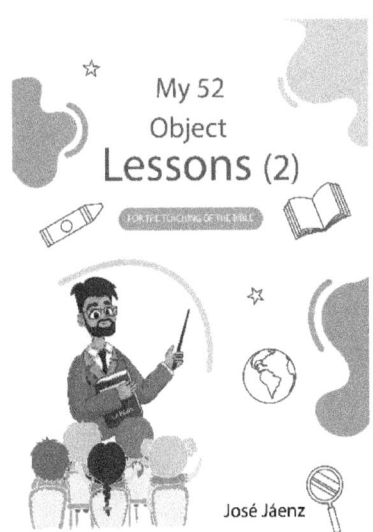

www.ingramcontent.com/pod-product-compliance
Lightning Source LLC
Chambersburg PA
CBHW070148230526
45471CB00002B/576